SPECTRUM®

Test Prep

Grade 3

Published by Spectrum®
An imprint of Carson-Dellosa Publishing LLC
Greensboro, North Carolina

Spectrum®
An imprint of Carson-Dellosa Publishing LLC
P.O. Box 35665
Greensboro, NC 27425 USA

ISBN 978-1-4838-1376-9

01-307157784

Table of Contents

What's Inside?

Spectrum Test Prep is designed to help you and your third grader prepare and plan for success on standardized tests.

Strategies

This workbook is structured around strategies. A strategy is a careful plan or method for achieving a particular goal, such as succeeding on a test. Strategies can be broad ways to approach a test as a whole or a category of skills. Strategies can also be specific, providing step-by-step instructions on how to tackle a problem or offering guidelines on how to answer a question about a story. Learning how to apply a strategy gives test-takers a plan for how to approach a test as a whole and how to answer questions.

This workbook offers a set of broader strategies and very specific strategies. General test-taking strategies apply to all tests, and should be used to help prepare for the test. Specific strategies for English Language Arts and Mathematics tests are divided into larger categories of skills students will encounter, such as reading literature or performing calculations. On each practice page, you will find even more specific strategies that apply to the skills.

Test Tips

Test Tips are included throughout the practice page. While strategies offer a plan for answering test items, Test Tips offer ideas for how to apply each strategy or how to approach a type of question. There are Test Tips that apply to all tests and Test Tips for English Language Arts and Mathematics tests.

Practice Pages

The workbook is divided into two sections, English Language Arts and Mathematics. Each section has practice activities that have questions similar to those that will appear on standardized tests. Also included are strategies and Test Tips to guide students. Students should use a pencil to complete these activities.

Strategy Review Pages

Strategy review pages give your student an opportunity to review and practice important strategies in each content area. These strategies cover the important skills students will encounter on tests in English Language Arts and Mathematics.

Answer Key

Answers for all of the practice pages and strategy review pages are found in an answer key at the end of the book.

Test-Taking Strategies

Being prepared is key to doing your best on test day. Read the tips below to help you prepare for tests.

In the days before the test...

- Keep up on your reading, worksheets, and assignments. Completing all your assigned work will help you be better prepared for the test.

- Don't wait until right before the test to review materials. Create a study schedule for the best result. That way, you can study a bit at a time and not all at once.

- Take advantage of sample items and practice tests. Complete these to practice for your test. If you run into concepts or skills that are new, ask a teacher or other adult.

The night before the test...

- Don't try to study everything all over again. If you've been studying in the days before the test, all you need the night before is a light review of your notes. Remind yourself of the key ideas and practice a few skills, but don't study late into the night.

- Make sure you have all the materials you will need for the test, such as pencils, paper, and a calculator. Check with your teacher to make sure you know what tools to bring. Having everything ready the night before will make the morning less stressful.

- Get a good night's sleep the night before the test. If you are well rested, you will be more alert and able to do your best.

On the day of the test...

- Don't skip breakfast. If you are hungry, you won't be thinking about the test. You'll be thinking about lunch.

- Make sure you have at least two sharpened pencils with you and any other tools needed.

- Read all directions carefully. Make sure you understand how you are supposed to answer each question.

- For multiple choice questions, read all the possible answers before choosing one. If you know that some answers are wrong, cross them off. Even if you have to guess, this will eliminate some wrong answers.

- Once you choose or write an answer, double check it by reading the question again. Confirm that your answer is correct.

- Answer every part of a question. If a question asks you to show your work or to explain how you arrived at an answer, make sure you include that information.

- If you are stuck on a question, or are unsure, mark it lightly with a pencil and move on. If you have time, you can come back. This is especially true on a timed test.

- Breathe! Remind yourself that you've prepared for the test and that you will do your best!

Strategies for English Language Arts Tests

Read the strategies below to learn more about how they work.

Use details from a story or passage to show your understanding.
Authors choose details to include in their writing. Every detail is important. As you read, look for details. Think about why the author chose those details. Use them to understand what the author means.

Use details to make a picture in your mind as you read.
Authors use descriptive details to paint a picture for readers. As you read, try to picture in your mind what people, places, and events look like.

Look carefully at pictures.
Authors include pictures, photos, and text features like charts and webs to show something about the words on the page. As you read, use them to help you understand what you are reading.

Reread to answer questions.
If you don't know the answer to a question right away, don't worry! You can go back and read the story or passage again. As you reread, look for the answer to the question.

Ask questions as you read.
Careful readers stop once in a while to think about what they are reading. They ask questions like, *What was this paragraph about?* As you read, ask yourself questions to make sure you understand.

Pay attention to how parts of a story or passage connect and fit together.
Authors work hard to make sure the parts of their writing fit together. In a story, the characters, place, and events fit together. In nonfiction, authors usually keep connected ideas together.

When you write, use details to support main ideas.
If you write a story, include details that help the reader see, smell, and hear the characters, places, and events. If you write nonfiction, use details to support a main idea.

Plan your writing.
Make a plan before you start writing. For stories, make sure you choose characters, a setting, and events. Your story should have a beginning, middle, and end. For nonfiction, choose main ideas. Usually one to three main ideas is enough. Then, support each main idea with details that help explain.

Revise to make sure your writing makes sense. Then, edit to fix errors. Use what you know about nouns, verbs, adjectives, and adverbs to make correct choices when you edit.
After you finish your draft, you may have time to revise and edit. First, revise to make sure your words say what you want them to say. Then, check spelling, capitalization, punctuation, and grammar to catch and fix errors.

English Language Arts

Ask and Answer Questions
Reading: Literature

DIRECTIONS: Read the story. Then, choose or write the best answer.

adapted from *Black Beauty* by Anna Sewell

One day, when there was a good deal of kicking in the meadow, my mother whinnied to me to come to her. "I wish you to pay attention to what I am about to say. The colts who live here are very good colts, but they are cart-horse colts. They have not learned manners.

"You have been well-bred and wellborn. Your father has a great name in these parts. Your grandfather won the cup two years in a row at the Newmarket Races. Your grandmother had the sweetest temper of any horse I have ever known. I think you have never seen me kick or bite. I hope you will grow up gentle and good and never follow bad ways. Do your work with goodwill, lift your legs up high when you trot, and never kick or bite, even in play."

Strategy — Find answers to questions you have about the story by looking back at the story. Find answers stated directly in the story.

Test Tip — Ask questions as you read to make sure you understand what is happening in the story.

1. **What did Black Beauty's mother say about each of his family members to prove he was "well-bred and wellborn"?**

   His father

   _____

   His grandfather

   _____

   His grandmother

   _____

   His mother

   _____

2. **In your own words, write what you think "well-bred and wellborn" means.**

   _____

   _____

3. **Select the word that best describes the attitude of Black Beauty's mother.**
   - (A) proud
   - (B) angry
   - (C) sad
   - (D) carefree

   Write how you know.

   _____

4. **Why does Black Beauty's mother tell Black Beauty that the other colts have not learned manners?**

   _____

   _____

5. **What does it mean when Black Beauty's mother says "do your work with goodwill"?**
   - (A) Work quickly and poorly.
   - (B) Work many hours.
   - (C) Work happily and well.
   - (D) Work as little as possible.

English Language Arts

English Language Arts

Ask and Answer Questions
Reading: Literature

DIRECTIONS: Read the story. Then, choose or write the best answer.

> **"The Fence" from *The Adventures of Tom Sawyer* by Mark Twain**
> Saturday morning was come, and all the summer world was bright and fresh, and brimming with life. There was a song in every heart . . . there was cheer in every face and a spring in every step. Tom appeared on the sidewalk with a bucket of whitewash and a long-handled brush. He surveyed the fence, and all gladness left him and a deep sadness settled down on his spirit. Thirty yards of board fence nine feet high. Life to him seemed hollow, and existence but a burden. Sighing, he dipped his brush and passed it along the topmost plank; repeated the operation; did it again; compared the small streak with the far-reaching continent of fence, and sat down on a tree-box discouraged.

Strategy   Read the story carefully, paying attention to details. Use exactly what the story says to answer questions.

Test Tip   Many stories have problems that the characters must solve. Look for details about a problem to help you understand the story.

1. **What is the main problem in the story?**
   (A) Tom did not know how to sing.
   (B) Tom needed another bucket.
   (C) Tom's brush was not long enough.
   (D) Tom did not want to paint the fence.

2. **What does the word "whitewash" mean?**
   (A) soap and water
   (B) white paint
   (C) cleaning solution
   (D) snow in the face

3. **How were Tom's feelings about Saturday different from the feelings of those around him?**

   _____

4. **Why do you think Tom sat down after painting just one small streak?**
   (A) He was tired.
   (B) He was overwhelmed.
   (C) He was lazy.
   (D) He was finished.

Choose two details from the story to support your answer to the question above.
   (A) "all gladness left him"
   (B) "the far-reaching continent of fence"
   (C) "Thirty yards of board fence"
   (D) "a deep sadness settled down"

5. **Why is Tom "discouraged" at the end of the story?**

   _____

   _____

6. **Which word in the story shows how Tom feels?**
   (A) sighing
   (B) cheer
   (C) surveyed
   (D) bright

Write how you know.

   _____

   _____

English Language Arts

Recount Stories and Determine Theme
Reading: Literature

DIRECTIONS: Read the story. Then, choose or write the best answer.

> **The Fox and the Grapes** *by Aesop*
> One warm summer day, a fox was walking along when he saw a bunch of grapes on a vine above him. Cool, juicy grapes would taste so good. The more he thought about it, the more the fox wanted those grapes. He tried standing on his tiptoes. He tried jumping high in the air. He tried getting a running start before he jumped. But no matter what he tried, the fox could not reach the grapes. As he angrily walked away, the fox muttered, "They were probably sour anyway!" Moral: A person (or fox) sometimes pretends that he does not want something he cannot have.

Strategy — Find the central message or main idea in a story by putting all of the details in the story together.

Test Tip — Fables are stories that have lessons called *morals*. A moral is a lesson that teaches people how to act. The moral is the main idea of a fable.

1. **These events from the story are out of order. Write the numbers 2, 3, 4, 5, 6, and 7 to retell the story in the correct order.**

   [1] One warm summer day, a fox was walking along.

   [ ] He tried standing on his tiptoes.

   [ ] No matter what he tried, the fox could not get the grapes.

   [ ] He saw a bunch of grapes on a vine above him.

   [ ] He tried jumping to get the grapes.

   [ ] The fox thought cool, juicy grapes would taste good.

   [ ] He walked away angrily.

   [8] The fox muttered, "They were probably sour anyway!"

2. **In your own words, state the lesson of this story.**

   _____

   _____

3. **Which detail supports the story's lesson?**
   - (A) "fox wanted those grapes"
   - (B) "he saw a bunch of grapes"
   - (C) "grapes would taste so good"
   - (D) "They were probably sour"

4. **Why did the fox say, "They were probably sour anyway"?**
   - (A) The grapes did not look ripe.
   - (B) The grapes were all wrinkled.
   - (C) He couldn't reach them.
   - (D) He tasted one, and it was sour.

5. **In your own words, retell the fable.**

   _____

   _____

   _____

   _____

   _____

   _____

English Language Arts

Recount Stories and Determine Theme
Reading: Literature

DIRECTIONS: Read the story. Then, choose or write the best answer.

Why the Sun and the Moon Live in the Sky
—Ghana folktale

Many, many years ago, the Sun and the Moon lived together on the earth. Water was their best friend, and they often came to see him. But Water never went to see the Sun and the Moon in their house. The Sun asked Water why he didn't visit. Water answered that he had too many friends and was afraid there would be no place for them in the Sun's house. So, the Sun built a very big house and then asked Water to come to him. Water came with all the fish and water animals. Soon, Water was up to the Sun's head and came higher and higher with all the fish and water animals. At last, Water was so high in the house that the Sun and the Moon went to the roof and sat there. Water soon came up onto the roof. What could the Sun and the Moon do? Where could they sit? They went up to the sky. They liked the place and began to live there.

Strategy | Read the story and then retell the story in your own words. Retelling a story will help you know if you understand it or if you need to reread.

Test Tip | Folktales are stories that tell how things began in nature. The main idea of a folktale is usually how something began to happen.

1. **These events from the story are out of order. Write the numbers 2, 3, 4, 5, 6, and 7 to retell the story in the correct order.**

   | 1 | Sun and Moon lived together on Earth.

   | | Water soon came up to the roof.

   | | Water did not think he would fit in the house.

   | | Sun and Moon went up to the sky.

   | | Water was their best friend, but he didn't visit.

   | | Sun built a very big house.

   | | Water came to visit with all his friends.

   | 8 | Sun and Moon began to live in the sky.

2. **What is the main idea of this folktale?**

   (A) never invite Water to visit

   (B) Water has many friends

   (C) how fish and water animals live in oceans

   (D) how the Sun and Moon came to be in the sky

   Write how you know.

   _____

3. **Choose two details to support the main idea that you chose in question 2.**

   (A) "Water soon came up onto the roof"

   (B) "Water was their best friend"

   (C) "Water had too many friends"

   (D) "Water was up to the Sun's head"

4. **Write the detail that explains why Water would not fit in Sun and Moon's house.**

   _____

   _____

5. **Retell the story in your own words.**

   _____

   _____

   _____

6. **How do you know this is a folktale?**

   _____

Name _____   Date _____

Describe Characters and Their Actions
Reading: Literature

DIRECTIONS: Read the story. Then, choose or write the best answer.

A Bumpy Ride

I wasn't very nervous when we first climbed into the car and strapped on our safety belts. I was sitting right next to my big brother. He had done this many times before. As we started to climb the hill, however, I could feel my heart jump into my throat.

"Brian?" I asked nervously. "Is this supposed to be so noisy?"

"Sure, Matthew," Brian answered. "It always does that."

A minute later, we were going so fast down the hill I didn't have time to think. A twist! A loop! A bunch of fast turns! Everyone around me screamed in delight. No wonder this was one of the most popular rides in the park. By the time the car pulled into the station and we got off the ride, I was ready to do it again!

Strategy As you read a story, look for details that describe characters—what they look like, what they think, how they feel, and what they do.

Test Tip Stories and passages often give details that tell how characters feel. Look for words that describe feelings as you read.

1. **What are Matthew and his brother doing in the story?**

   _____

   Write how you know.

   _____

   _____

2. **Why did Matthew's heart jump into his throat?**

   _____

   _____

3. **How are Matthew and his brother different?**

   (A) Matthew was nervous; his brother was not.

   (B) Matthew's brother was nervous; Matthew was not.

   (C) Matthew's brother hates roller coasters, Matthew does not.

   (D) Matthew loved roller coasters; his brother did not.

4. **How did Matthew change at the end of the story?**

   _____

   _____

   Write how you know.

   _____

   _____

5. **Which two sentences best describe the character Matthew?**

   (A) He is willing to try new things.

   (B) He is not close with his brother.

   (C) He is afraid of new experiences.

   (D) He likes to do what his brother does.

6. **Would Matthew have gone on the bumpy ride if his brother weren't with him? Write how you know.**

   _____

English Language Arts

Describe Characters and Their Actions
Reading: Literature

The Contest

Jin and Jo loved to enter contests. It did not matter what the prize was. Once, they wrote a poem for a magazine contest. They won a free copy of the magazine. Another time, they correctly guessed how many marbles were in a glass jar. They got to take all the marbles home with them. One morning, Jin was reading the Crunchy Munchies cereal box as he ate his breakfast.

"Jo," he said, "here's another contest! The first-place winner gets a bike. Second prize is a tent."

"Those are great prizes," said Jo. "How do we enter?"

The box said that the boys had to fill out a box top with their names and address. The more box tops they filled out, the better their chances for winning the drawing. Jin and Jo started eating Crunchy Munchies every morning. They also asked everyone they knew for cereal box tops. By the end of four weeks, Jin and Jo had sixteen box tops to send in for the drawing.

"I'm glad that's over," said Jin. "If I had to look at another box of that stuff, I don't know what I'd do."

A few weeks passed. One day, the boys got a letter in the mail.

"Hooray! We've won third prize in the Crunchy Munchies contest!" Jo exclaimed. "I didn't even know there was a third prize."

Jin took the letter and started to read. His smile disappeared. "Oh, no!" he cried. "Third prize is a year's supply of Crunchy Munchies!"

Strategy Tell what characters do or what happens to them by looking for details in the story as you read.

Test Tip Characters have reasons for why they act the way they do. Look for details in the story that explain why characters think, say, or do something.

1. **What is this story about?**

   (A) two teachers who love cereal

   (B) two cereal makers who love contests

   (C) two sisters who play marbles

   (D) two brothers who love contests

2. **Why did Jin and Jo enter the Crunchy Munchies contest?**

   _____

   _____

3. **What two actions do Jin and Jo take to try to win the contest?**

   (A) They ate Crunchy Munchies every morning.

   (B) They read the contest rules in a magazine.

   (C) They asked everyone for cereal box tops.

   (D) They read the Crunchy Munchies cereal box.

4. **What are Jin and Jo's feelings at the end of the story? Write how you know.**

   _____

   _____

5. **Why does Jin's smile disappear at the end of the story?**

   (A) Jin and Jo can't figure out how to enter the contest.

   (B) Jin and Jo ate so much cereal they don't want the prize.

   (C) Jin and Jo don't collect enough box tops to win.

   (D) Jin and Jo argue about who will get the prize.

6. **Do you think Jin and Jo would have entered the contest if they knew what third prize would be? Provide details to explain your answer.**

   _____

English Language Arts

Understand Literal and Nonliteral Language
Reading: Literature

DIRECTIONS: Read the poem. Then, choose or write the best answer.

My Bed Is a Boat *by Robert Louis Stevenson*

My bed is like a little boat;
　　Nurse helps me in when I [1]embark;
She [2]girds me in my sailor's coat
　　And starts me in the dark.

At night, I go on board and say
　　Good night to all my friends on shore;
I shut my eyes and sail away
　　And see and hear no more.

And sometimes things to bed I take,
　　As [3]prudent sailors have to do;
Perhaps a slice of wedding-cake,
　　Perhaps a toy or two.

All night across the dark we steer:
　　But when the day returns at last
Safe in my room, beside the pier,
　　I find my [4]vessel fast.

　　[1] *embarks*—go on board a boat
　　[2] *girds*—dresses
　　[3] *prudent*—careful
　　[4] *vessel*—ship or large boat

Strategy

As you read, determine the meaning of words and phrases in the story, poem, or passage.

Test Tip

Nonliteral words and phrases can compare two things that are not usually compared. For example: *The dog was the size of a tank. His knee swelled up like a balloon after he fell.*

1. What does the speaker, or poem's narrator, compare his bed to?

_____

Write two words or phrases from the poem that are details that support the comparison.

_____

_____

2. Read the lines from the poem below.
"I shut my eyes and sail away
And see and hear no more."
How do these lines give a detail about a bed like a boat?

Ⓐ Sailors see people when they sail.

Ⓑ Boats are silent on the water.

Ⓒ The speaker is going to sleep.

Ⓓ It is night so there is nothing to see.

3. Does the speaker of the poem really "sail away"? Determine if this is literal or nonliteral language to explain your answer.

_____

_____

4. Which sentence matches the meaning of the lines from the poem below?
"Nurse helps me in when I embark;
She girds me in my sailor's coat
And starts me in the dark"

Ⓐ The night nurse helps the speaker with his coat before taking him to the boat.

Ⓑ The speaker's nanny helps him into bed, pulling the blankets over him.

Ⓒ They are at a hospital because the speaker is sick and needs care.

Ⓓ The nanny helps the speaker on the boat and sails with him.

English Language Arts

Understand Literal and Nonliteral Language
Reading: Literature

DIRECTIONS: Read the story. Then, choose or write the best answer.

The Kite

It was the most tiresome kite in the world, always wagging its tail, shaking its ears, breaking its string, sitting down on the tops of houses, getting stuck in trees, entangled in hedges, flopping down on ponds, or lying flat on the grass, and refusing to rise higher than a yard from the ground.

I have often sat and thought about that kite, and wondered who its father and mother were. Perhaps they were very poor people, just made of newspaper and little bits of common string knotted together, obliged to fly day and night for a living, and never able to give any time to their children or to bring them up properly. It was pretty, for it had a snow-white face, and pink and white ears. And, with these, no one, let alone a kite, could help being pretty. But though the kite was pretty, it was not good, and it did not prosper. It came to a bad end, oh! a terrible end indeed. It stuck itself on a roof one day, a common red roof with a broken chimney and three tiles missing. It stuck itself there, and it would not move. The children tugged and pulled and coaxed and cried, but still it would not move. At last they fetched a ladder, and had nearly reached it when suddenly the kite started and flew away. Right away over the field and over the heath, and over the far, far woods, and it never came back again—never—never.

Dear, that is all. But I think sometimes that perhaps beyond the dark pines and the roaring sea the kite is flying still, on and on, farther and farther away, forever and forever.

Strategy

Try using the dictionary definition of a word or phrase—the literal meaning—to see if that meaning makes sense. If it doesn't make sense, find a nonliteral meaning.

Test Tip

Authors sometimes give human characteristics to a thing, idea, or animal. This is nonliteral language called *personification*. Look for details that give human qualities, such as feelings.

1. **Which three details support the idea that the kite was "the most tiresome kite in the world"?**

   (A) shaking its ears

   (B) refusing to rise higher

   (C) falling off of a roof

   (D) wagging its tail

   (E) fetching a ladder

   (F) prospering and good

2. **Does the kite actually do all of the things described in the first paragraph? Write how you know.**

   _____

   _____

3. **Describe what the kite looks like using details from the story.**

   _____

   Which detail describing the kite is an example of nonliteral language? Write how you know.

   _____

4. **Why does the author wonder who the kite's parents are?**

   (A) to thank them for the kite

   (B) to find more kites like this kite

   (C) to understand the kite's bad behavior

   (D) to ask them to coax the kite off the roof

English Language Arts

Identify Parts of Text
Reading: Literature

DIRECTIONS: Read the poem. Then, choose or write the best answer.

Spring Garden
Trees tap at my window
And tell me to come
Out to the garden
Where the wind plays and hums.

Small green buds whisper
Secrets to me
Of spring coming soon
And of flowers yet to be.

I go to the window
And open it wide.
Now the trees shout,
"Please come on outside!"

With a smile on my face,
I race out the door.
I look up at the trees,
Which are swaying once more.

Strategy

Identify the parts of stories (paragraphs), plays (scenes), and poems (stanzas) to understand how all the parts fit together.

Test Tip

Poems have stanzas, which are similar to paragraphs in stories. Most poems have more than one stanza. Each stanza builds on the previous stanza, which means that all the stanzas are connected in some way.

1. **What happens in the beginning of the poem (Stanza 1)?**
   (A) The window opens on a windy day.
   (B) The wind hums against the window.
   (C) The trees invite the speaker to the garden.
   (D) The speaker plays outside on a windy day.

Write the lines from the poem that helped you answer the question above.

_____

_____

2. **In which stanza does the poet tell you that spring is coming soon?**
   (A) Stanza 1
   (B) Stanza 2
   (C) Stanza 3
   (D) Stanza 4

3. **In the second stanza, what clues to spring does the poet see?**

_____

4. **In the third stanza, what phrase uses nonliteral language?**

_____

_____

Write what you think this phrase means in the poem.

_____

_____

5. **How does each stanza build on the one before?**
   (A) Each stanza repeats the one before.
   (B) Each stanza continues the story from the one before.
   (C) Each stanza rhymes the same as the one before.
   (D) The stanzas are not related at all.

English Language Arts

Identify Parts of Text
Reading: Literature

DIRECTIONS: Read the poem. Then, choose or write the best answer.

"My Shadow" by Robert Louis Stevenson

I have a little shadow that goes in and out with me,
And what can be the use of him is more than I can see.
He is very, very like me, from the heels up to the head;
And I see him jump before me, when I jump into my bed.
The funniest thing about him is the way he likes to grow—
Not at all like proper children, which is always very slow;
For he sometimes shoots up taller, like an india-rubber ball,
And he sometimes gets so little that there's none of him at all.

He hasn't got a [1]notion of how children ought to play,
And can only make a fool of me in every sort of way.
He stays so close beside me, he's a coward you can see;
I'd [2]think shame to stick to nursie as that shadow sticks to me!
One morning, very early, before the sun was up,
I 'rose and found the shining dew on every buttercup;
But my lazy little shadow, like an [3]arrant sleepy head,
Had stayed at home behind me and was fast asleep in bed.

[1] *notion*—idea, understanding
[2] *think shame to stick to nursie*—be embarrassed to stay close to my nanny
[3] *arrant*—complete, extreme

Strategy

Figure out the meaning of the other stanzas in a poem by using what you know about the first stanza.

Test Tip

Remember that poems have stanzas that build on each other. Poems are about one topic or theme, just like stories. Think about what a poem is mainly about to understand it better.

1. What is the poet describing?

- (A) playing
- (B) his shadow
- (C) sleeping
- (D) morning

2. Write one line that tells you what the poem is about.

_____

_____

3. Which sentence best describes how the two stanzas build on each other?

- (A) Stanza 1 describes why shadows exist. Stanza 2 continues that explanation.
- (B) Stanza 1 is about the speaker's fear of shadows. Stanza 2 gives reasons for that fear.
- (C) Stanza 1 explains what a shadow is. Stanza 2 explains what shadows do.
- (D) Stanza 1 tells about how the shadow looks. Stanza 2 tells how the shadow acts.

4. Write two lines from the poem that show that the speaker is bothered by his shadow.

_____

_____

_____

_____

_____

English Language Arts

Identify Points of View
Reading: Literature

DIRECTIONS: Read each paragraph. Then, choose or write the best answer.

A Sad Tale

A. I felt sorry for Jason when I saw him come in this morning. He looked so sad. I could tell he had a hard time focusing in class. When it was finally time for recess, I asked him to stay behind. Then, he told me his problem. With one quick phone call, the problem was solved.

B. I was in such a rush this morning that I forgot the permission form for the school field trip. The class was going to a museum that had a life-sized dinosaur skeleton. Mom had even reminded me that today was the last day to turn it in. And now I would miss it! At recess, Ms. Warner asked me what was wrong. Then, she made a phone call, and Mom soon brought the form to school.

C. As soon as Jason left for the bus, I saw his permission form sitting on the counter. I had planned to bring it to school anyway. I couldn't let Jason miss a chance to see dinosaurs—they are his favorite things! I was glad that Ms. Warner called and told Jason I was on my way. Jason was so happy that he would be able to go to the dinosaur museum!

Strategy
As you read, identify the narrator, or who is telling the story, and note what he or she knows about characters and what is happening to them in the story.

Test Tip
A narrator may be a character in the story or the voice of someone outside the story. Point of view describes what characters and narrators know, think, or feel. First-person point of view is when the narrator is a character in the story. First-person point of view uses the word *I*. Narrators also share their thoughts and feelings.

1. Write who narrates, or tells the story, in each paragraph.

Paragraph A: _____

Paragraph B: _____

Paragraph C: _____

Write one detail you used to determine the narrators for each paragraph.

Paragraph A: _____

Paragraph B: _____

Paragraph C: _____

2. What is the problem that each narrator wants to solve in each paragraph?

Paragraph A: _____

Paragraph B: _____

Paragraph C: _____

3. Which narrator does not know the reason that Jason is sad?

_____

Explain why the narrator does not know.

_____

_____

_____

4. Which point of view is used in each paragraph?

_____

Write how you know.

_____

_____

English Language Arts

Identify Points of View
Reading: Literature

DIRECTIONS: Read the story. Then, choose or write the best answer.

Lunch Guests

It was a sunny spring day. Kaye and her friend, Tasha, were walking in the woods. As they walked, they noticed many squirrels ahead of them running in the same direction.

"Let's follow them and see where they are going," Kaye said.

"Great idea!" exclaimed Tasha, and the two girls raced ahead.

Soon, they came to a large clearing in the forest. There were hundreds and hundreds of squirrels. There were more squirrels than either girl had ever seen. They stared in amazement at the scene before them. Then, a plump gray squirrel with a fluffy tail skittered over to them and said politely, "Would you care to join us for lunch?"

Kaye and Tasha were stunned into silence. But after a moment, they looked at each other, shrugged, and said, "Why not?" They both liked nuts.

Strategy As you read a story, find clues about the point of view by identifying the narrator.

Test Tip A narrator may be a character in the story (first-person point of view) or the voice of someone who is not part of the story (third-person point of view). The narrator tells what happens and may tell what some or all of the characters think or feel.

1. **From whose point of view is this story told?**

   (A) Kaye's first-person point of view

   (B) Tasha's point of view

   (C) the squirrel's point of view

   (D) a narrator's third-person point of view

2. **Which two things does the story's narrator know?**

   (A) the setting of the story

   (B) what Tasha and Kaye think

   (C) the squirrels' thoughts

   (D) why the girls are friends

3. **Rewrite the first paragraph from Kaye's point of view.**

   _____

   _____

   _____

4. **How did Kaye and Tasha feel about a talking squirrel inviting them to lunch?**

   (A) scared

   (B) angry

   (C) stunned

   (D) jealous

   Write how you know.

   _____

   _____

   _____

   _____

5. **What would be different about the story if it were written in first-person point of view?**

   _____

   _____

English Language Arts

Compare and Contrast Stories
Reading: Literature

DIRECTIONS: Read the story. Then, choose or write the best answer.

Adapted from "The Ugly Duckling"
by Hans Christian Andersen

It was lovely summer weather in the country. In a sunny spot, a duck sat on her nest, watching for her young family to hatch. "Are you all hatched?" she asked. "No, the largest egg lies there still. I wonder how long this is to last, I am quite tired of it." Then, she seated herself again on the nest.

At last the large egg broke. A young one crept out crying, "Peep, peep." The duck stared at it and exclaimed, "It is very large and not at all like the others. I wonder if it is a turkey. We shall soon find it out."

The ducks made themselves comfortable in a farmyard. But the poor duckling was bitten and pushed and made fun of by all the animals. "He is too big," they all said. The poor little thing did not know where to go. He was quite miserable because he was so ugly and laughed at by the whole farmyard.

One evening, just as the sun set, a large flock of beautiful birds came out of the bushes. The duckling had never seen any like them before. They were swans, and they curved their graceful necks. Their soft feathers shone with dazzling whiteness. They uttered a cry as they spread their wings and flew away from that cold place to warmer countries across the sea.

The duckling found himself lying one morning in a swamp. He felt the warm sun shining, and saw that all around was beautiful spring. Then, the young bird felt that his wings were strong. He flapped them against his sides. He rose high into the air. He flew until he found himself in a large garden.

Everything looked beautiful, in the freshness of early spring. Three beautiful white swans came out of the bushes. They rustled their feathers and swam lightly over the smooth water. The duckling remembered the lovely birds, and felt more unhappy than ever.

"I will fly to those beautiful birds," he exclaimed.

Then, he flew to the water and swam towards the beautiful swans. The moment they saw him, they rushed to meet him with outstretched wings. He bent his head down to the surface of the water.

But what did he see in the clear stream below? His own image. He was no longer a dark, gray bird, ugly and disagreeable to look at. He was a graceful and beautiful swan. The great swans swam round him and stroked his neck with their beaks as a welcome.

Strategy | While reading, try to get a general idea of what it is about. Then, reread the story to focus on understanding the setting, plot, and theme.

Test Tip | The setting of a story is where the story takes place. A story's plot is what happens to the characters. The theme of a story is the story's main message or lesson—what the characters learn.

1. **Which sentence best describes the setting of the story?**

   (A) A shore by the ocean

   (B) A busy city park

   (C) A farm in the country

   (D) A crowded zoo

Write two details from the story that support your answer.

_____

_____

_____

_____

_____

Compare and Contrast Stories
Reading: Literature

DIRECTIONS: Determine the problem a character must solve or overcome by identifying the plot of a story.

Strategy | Determine the problem a character must solve or overcome by identifying the plot of a story.

Test Tip | Remember that a theme of a story is not the story's topic. A theme is an overall idea or message the story gives to readers.

2. Who is the main character in this story?

- (A) A large duckling
- (B) A beautiful tree
- (C) A flock of swans
- (D) A family of ducks

3. Write the problem that the biggest duckling needed to solve.

_____

_____

_____

4. Which two ways was the ugly duckling able to solve his problem?

- (A) He chose to run away, flying to another farmyard.
- (B) He decided to join the swans, swimming to them.
- (C) He grew into a graceful, white swan as time passed.
- (D) He began to tease the other ducklings.

5. Write a reason for how the swans behaved when the ugly duckling swam for them. Use details about the story's plot, or what happens to the characters in the story.

_____

_____

_____

_____

6. What is the best theme for the story?

- (A) Trying to change or grow for the better will never work.
- (B) All ugly creatures will grow up to be beautiful and loved.
- (C) Try not to look or act different from others or you will be teased.
- (D) It is okay to look different, because everyone is beautiful.

Write how you know.

_____

_____

_____

_____

7. What do you think the ugly duckling learned in the story?

_____

_____

_____

_____

English Language Arts

Compare and Contrast Stories
Reading: Literature

DIRECTIONS: Read the story. Then, choose or write the best answer.

Adapted from "The Emperor's New Suit"
by Hans Christian Andersen

Many years ago lived an emperor who thought so much of new clothes that he spent all his money to get them. His only goal was to be always well dressed. He had a coat for every hour of the day.

One day, two tricksters came to his city. They made people believe that they were weavers, and claimed they could weave the finest cloth. They said that their colors and patterns were not only beautiful, but the clothes made of their material had the power of being invisible to any man who was stupid or unfit for his job. "That must be wonderful cloth," thought the emperor. "If I were to be dressed in a suit made of this cloth, I would be able to find out which men in my empire were unfit for their jobs. And I could tell the clever from the stupid. I must have this cloth woven for me without delay."

The emperor gave a large sum of money to the crooks to make him a suit. They set up two looms and pretended to be very hard at work. But they did nothing whatever on the looms. They asked for the finest silk and the most precious gold-cloth. They hid everything they got, and worked at the empty looms till late at night.

At last, the emperor wished to see it himself. He went to the two clever crooks, who now worked as hard as they could, but without using any thread.

"Is it not wonderful?" said one of the emperor's men. "Your Majesty must admire the colors and the pattern."

And then, they pointed to the empty looms.

What is this? thought the emperor to himself. *I do not see anything at all.*

"Really," he said, turning to the weavers, "your cloth has our approval." All of the men who were with him looked and looked. Although they could not see anything, they said, "It is very beautiful." And they all advised him to wear the new clothes at a great parade, which was soon to take place.

The emperor marched in the parade. All who saw him in the street and out of the windows exclaimed, "Indeed, the emperor's new suit is unique! How well it fits him!" Nobody wished to let others know he saw nothing.

"But he has nothing on at all," said a little child at last. Soon, all the people cried, "But he has nothing on at all!"

The emperor heard this, but he thought, "Now I must continue to the end." And he walked with still greater dignity, as if he wore the most beautiful suit in the world.

Strategy

Identify the plot by asking yourself who is in the story and what happens to them. Understanding the plot will help you find the theme.

Test Tip

Look for similar themes in different stories that are repeated using different characters and plots. A popular theme in many stories is *Keep trying and you will succeed.*

1. **What is the plot of this story?**

   (A) The emperor is tricked into wearing nothing at a parade.

   (B) The tricksters helped the emperor fire people who were unfit.

   (C) The people prepared for a parade by buying clothes.

   (D) A cloth weaver uses very expensive cloth to make a suit.

   Write how you know.

   _____

   _____

   _____

English Language Arts

Compare and Contrast Stories
Reading: Literature

Strategy Compare two stories to learn more about plot, setting, and theme of each story.

Test Tip Stories written by the same author often have similar themes. Keep in mind that the themes might not be exactly the same, but have an idea in common.

2. **Why did the emperor's men pretend to see the cloth?**

  (A) They actually saw the new cloth.

  (B) The people were trying to trick the emperor.

  (C) They didn't want to disagree with the emperor.

  (D) They thought the cloth was beautiful.

Write how you know.

_____

_____

_____

3. **After the little child says the emperor is not wearing any clothes, the emperor walks "with still greater dignity". Why does the emperor do this?**

_____

_____

_____

4. **Which sentence describes the theme of this story?**

  (A) Never hire workers who promise you everything you want.

  (B) You will look foolish if you worry too much about appearance.

  (C) Trust the decisions of your leaders because they know best.

  (D) Make sure you look your best at all times, no matter the cost.

Write how you know.

_____

_____

_____

_____

5. **"The Ugly Duckling" and "The Emperor's New Clothes" are written by the same author. How are their themes similar? Look for details in each story about what the characters learn.**

_____

_____

_____

_____

6. **Which theme might apply to both "The Ugly Duckling" and "The Emperor's New Clothes"?**

  (A) It is okay to like beautiful things, but appearance isn't everything.

  (B) Only the most beautiful creatures and people get ahead in life.

  (C) Make sure you surround yourself with beauty at all times.

  (D) Try your best to be a beautiful person inside and out.

Write how you know.

_____

_____

_____

English Language Arts
Demonstrate Understanding of a Text
Reading: Informational Text

DIRECTIONS: Read the passage. Then, choose or write the best answer.

> **Quicksand**
> Stories of people and animals sinking into quicksand have been told for hundreds of years. While some of the stories may be true, it helps to understand what quicksand really is. Quicksand is a deep bed of light, loose sand that is full of water. It looks much like regular sand on the surface, but it is really very different. Regular sand is packed firmly and can be walked on. Quicksand is loose and full of water. It cannot support much weight. Quicksand usually forms around rivers and lakes. Water collects in the sand and does not drain away. It continues to collect until the sand becomes soft. Although some objects can float in quicksand, it cannot support the heavy weight of an animal or person.

Strategy Ask questions as you read to make sure you understand what is happening in the passage. Reread the passage to find the answers.

Test Tip Ask questions about the topic, the main idea, and the details.

1. **Write how quicksand and regular sand are different. Use details from the passage.**

   _____

   _____

2. **Which three words describe quicksand?**

   (A) wet

   (B) loose

   (C) soft

   (D) strong

   Write a sentence describing quicksand using the three words you chose.

   _____

   _____

3. **Write a question that uses the key detail, "Quicksand usually forms around rivers and lakes."**

   _____

4. **The passage says that stories of people and animals sinking into quicksand may be true. Which key detail would support this idea?**

   (A) "Stories of people and animals sinking into quicksand have been told for hundreds of years."

   (B) "It looks much like regular sand on the surface, but it is really very different."

   (C) "Quicksand usually forms around rivers and lakes."

   (D) "Although some objects can float in quicksand, it cannot support the heavy weight of an animal or person."

5. **What is a synonym for the word "support" in the last sentence?**

   (A) hold

   (B) care

   (C) upkeep

   (D) help

Demonstrate Understanding of a Text
Reading: Informational Text

DIRECTIONS: Read the passage. Then, choose or write the best answer.

Dynamite

Dynamite is one of the most powerful explosives in the world. It is often used to blast away earth. This is needed for building dams, making foundations for large buildings, and for mining. The word *dynamite* comes from a Greek word meaning "power". Alfred Nobel first produced dynamite in 1867. Nobel was a Swedish chemist. He later became famous for using his fortune to establish the Nobel Prizes. His first dynamite was dangerous to use because it exploded so easily. He later developed a safer mixture of chemicals and chalk-like soil. He placed this mixture into hollow tubes, or sticks. This stick dynamite was safer because it would not explode until a blasting cap was added. Nobel later invented special dynamite called *blasting gelatin*. This dynamite would explode under water. Today, there are over 200 kinds of dynamite.

Strategy Reread a passage several times to find answers to questions. If you focus on one question at time, it will be easier to find the answer.

Test Tip Keep the 5W questions in mind as you read: *Who, What, Where, Why, When*.

1. **Why is dynamite an important invention? Use details from the passage.**

_____

_____

2. **Which detail tells where the word "dynamite" comes from?**

   (A) "Dynamite is one of the most powerful explosives in the world."

   (B) "The word *dynamite* comes from a Greek word meaning 'power'."

   (C) "Alfred Nobel first produced dynamite in 1867."

   (D) "Today, there are over 200 kinds of dynamite."

3. **Use details from the passage to explain why Nobel would have used the word "dynamite" for his invention.**

_____

_____

_____

4. **Write a question that uses the key detail, "He later developed a safer mixture of chemicals and chalk-like soil."**

_____

_____

5. **What is the main idea of this passage?**

   (A) Dynamite was an important invention that was made safer.

   (B) Alfred Nobel used his fortunes to award prizes.

   (C) The first dynamite made was dangerous.

   (D) Inventing dynamite was a quick and easy process.

Write two details that support the main idea you chose.

_____

_____

Determine Main Idea
Reading: Informational Text

DIRECTIONS: Read the passage. Then, choose or write the best answer.

Marie Curie

One of the greatest scientists of all time is Marie Curie. Marie Curie was born in Poland in 1867. She studied at a university in Paris and lived in France for most of her adult life. Along with her husband, she studied radioactivity. Radioactivity is what happens to atoms when they quickly break down. Radiation, the energy sent out by the atom as it breaks down, can be very dangerous to people and animals. Marie Curie was awarded the Nobel Prize in chemistry in 1911 for her work discovering radium and polonium, two radioactive elements. Some medical advances are based on the research of the Marie Curie and her husband. They include the X-ray and the use of radiation to treat cancer.

The Curies were both generous people. Even though they were poor for most of their lives, they did not patent, or keep the rights to, any of their discoveries. They wanted everyone to benefit from their research. Marie Curie died in 1934. The world should not forget her.

Strategy | Use the details in a passage to identify the main idea. Put all of the details together and see what idea they are mostly about.

Test Tip | Keep the 5W questions in mind as you read: *Who, What, Where, Why, When.* Finding answers to these questions will help you find the main idea.

1. **Write three details from the passage that support the main idea below.**

Main Idea	One of the greatest scientists of all time is Marie Curie.
Detail 1:	
Detail 2:	
Detail 3:	

2. **Which key details support the idea that the Curies were generous? Choose all that apply.**

   (A) They were poor for most of their lives.

   (B) They did not keep the rights to their discoveries.

   (C) They wanted everyone to have their research.

   (D) They studied radioactivity and chemistry.

3. **What is radioactivity? Use details from the passage.**

_____

_____

4. **What modern technologies may not exist if it weren't for Marie Curie and her husband? Choose all that apply.**

   (A) cars

   (B) X-ray

   (C) vaccines

   (D) cancer treatments

5. **How does the author of the passage feel about Marie Curie? Use details from the passage.**

_____

_____

Determine Main Idea
Reading: Informational Text

DIRECTIONS: Read each passage carefully. Then, choose the best answer for the question.

Insects in Winter

In the summertime, insects can be seen buzzing and fluttering around us. But as winter's cold weather begins, the insects seem to disappear. Do you know where they go? Many insects find a warm place to spend the winter.

Ants try to dig deep into the ground. Some beetles stack up in piles under rocks or dead leaves. Female grasshoppers don't even stay around for winter. In the fall, they lay their eggs and die. The eggs hatch in the spring.

Bees also try to protect themselves from the winter cold. Honeybees gather in a ball in the middle of their hive. The bees stay in this tight ball trying to stay warm. Winter is very hard for insects, but each spring the survivors come out and the buzzing and fluttering begins again.

Strategy — Look for at least two details that support the main idea you have found. If you can't find supporting details, find a new main idea.

Test Tip — Remember that every main idea has details that support it. Reread the passage and look for details that lead to a main idea.

1. **Use the passage to fill in the main idea below. Fill in the rest of the ovals with supporting details.**

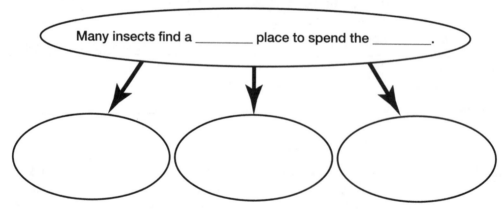

Many insects find a _____ place to spend the _____.

2. **Why doesn't the author mention how animals survive in the winter? Use the main idea to answer.**

_____

_____

3. **How are bees and beetles similar in the way they try to protect themselves in the winter?**

_____

_____

4. **How do the details support the main idea?**

   (A) The details are about how animals hibernate.

   (B) The details are about the different kinds of insects.

   (C) The details are about what insects do to survive winter.

   (D) The details are about insects that die in the winter.

Name _____   Date _____

English Language Arts

Describe Relationships in Texts
Reading: Informational Text

DIRECTIONS: Read the passage. Then, choose or write the best answer.

The Great Ice Age

Long ago, the climate of the earth began to cool. As the temperature dropped, giant sheets of ice, called *glaciers*, moved across the land. As time went on, snow and ice covered many forests and grasslands. Some plants and animals could not survive the changes in the climate. Other animals moved to warmer land. But some animals were able to adapt. They learned to live with the cold and snowy weather because they changed. Finally, the earth's temperature began to rise. The ice and snow began to melt. Today, the land at the North and South Poles is a reminder of the Great Ice Age.

Strategy   List all of the ideas or events in a passage. Then, determine how each idea or event is connected, or fits together in the passage.

Test Tip   Authors use words to connect ideas. Sometimes, authors use words about time (*first, next, last*) or about cause and effect (*because, then, so*).

1. Use the graphic organizer to list the events of the Great Ice Age in order. Use details from the passage.

1. The climate of the earth began to cool.
2.
3.
4. Many plants and animals died.
5.
6.
7. The earth's temperature began to rise.
8.

2. Write at least two words that connect ideas. Look for words about time or cause and effect.

_____

_____

_____

3. According to the passage, what does "glaciers" mean?

_____

4. Why did the author say that the land at the North and South Poles is a reminder of the Great Ice Age?

_____

_____

5. What happened to plants and animals that could not adapt to or escape the new climate?

_____

6. During the Great Ice Age, did snow and ice cover all of the earth? Explain, using details from the passage.

_____

_____

_____

_____

English Language Arts

Describe Relationships in Texts
Reading: Informational Text

DIRECTIONS: Read the passage. Then, choose or write the best answer.

Tornadoes and Hurricanes

It is easy to see why people get hurricanes and tornadoes mixed up. Both are strong storms that have high winds. They both can cause a large amount of damage. Hurricanes and tornadoes can both appear in either the Northern or Southern hemispheres. Hurricanes and tornadoes rotate differently in each hemisphere. South of the equator, they rotate clockwise. North of the equator, they rotate counterclockwise. However, they are different in some ways.

Tornadoes originate, or begin, from strong thunderstorms. They extend down to the ground. They are funnel-shaped and are very hard to predict. In the United States, there are about 1,000 tornadoes reported each year. Tornadoes can have wind speeds up to 300 miles per hour. Because of this high wind, these storms can pull trees out of the ground and send cars flying hundreds of yards into the air. A tornado usually moves about 30 miles per hour. Tornadoes can last several seconds or over an hour.

Hurricanes, on the other hand, form over the ocean. A hurricane can be up to 600 miles across and make winds up to 200 miles per hour. Each hurricane usually lasts for over a week. They move 10 to 20 miles per hour. When a hurricane reaches land, it can cause huge storm surges with heavy rains. A storm surge is when a storm along a coastline causes the tide to rise to very high levels. This causes flooding. Hurricanes can be predicted and tracked.

While both tornadoes and hurricanes are large storms that can cause major damage, they each have their own features.

Strategy   Compare two or more ideas to see how they are connected. Look for how an idea builds on the previous idea.

Test Tip   In addition to words about time or about cause and effect, authors also describe ideas by comparing and contrasting them. Look for words such as *however, on the other hand,* or *both.*

1. **How are the ideas in this passage connected?**

   Ⓐ sequence of events

   Ⓑ cause and effect

   Ⓒ compare and contrast

   Ⓓ time order

   Which words does the author use to connect ideas?

   _____

2. **According to the passage, what causes a tornado?**

   Ⓐ a storm over the ocean

   Ⓑ high winds

   Ⓒ storm surges

   Ⓓ strong thunderstorms

3. **Complete the Venn diagram about tornadoes and hurricanes. Use details from the passage.**

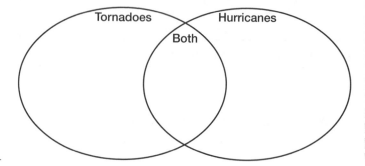

4. **Why does the author discuss two ideas—hurricanes and tornadoes? Explain how the two ideas are connected.**

   _____

   _____

Name _____ Date _____

Describe Connections
Reading: Informational Text

DIRECTIONS: Read the passage. Then, choose or write the best answer.

Jobs During World War II

World War II changed the way people of the United States lived and worked. On December 7, 1941, the Japanese attacked Pearl Harbor, Hawaii. Because of this, the United States entered World War II. The shift in the way Americans lived and worked seemed to change overnight.

Before World War II, the United States was recovering from the Great Depression. The Great Depression was a time when people had very little money. Many people were out of work. The United States government had been focusing on the problems here rather than problems in other countries. Most workers in the United States were men. Women usually took care of children and the home.

After the attack on Pearl Harbor, thousands of men joined the armed forces to fight the war. Women had to take jobs to help win the war. Men had performed these jobs. Women became welders, electricians, and factory workers. The number of women in the work place almost doubled during this time. Because more Americans had jobs during the war, people's lives began to improve.

Strategy — Identify clue words in sentences to understand how an author connects sentences and paragraphs.

Test Tip — An author may write sentences that compare, show cause and effect, or sequence. Words such as *before, after,* and *during* show sequence (time) and show comparison (something happened before or after an event).

1. **What is the author's opinion about the effect of World War II on the people of the United States?**

   (A) The author thinks the war was bad for the people of the United States.

   (B) The author thinks the war was good for the people of the United States.

   (C) The author thinks the war had no effect on the people of the United States.

   (D) The author thinks women should not have gone to work during the war.

2. **What caused the United States to enter the war?**

   _____

   Write the key detail that helped you answer the question.

   _____

   _____

3. **Why did more women go to work after December of 1941?**

   (A) They were tired of not earning their own money.

   (B) The government wanted them to join the armed forces.

   (C) There were not enough men at home to do the work.

   (D) They were tired of taking care of children and homes.

4. **The main idea of this passage is, "World War II changed the way people of the United States lived and worked." Write three details to support this main idea.**

   _____

   _____

5. **What is your opinion on the effect of World War II on the people of the United States?**

   _____

   _____

Describe Connections

Reading: Informational Text

DIRECTIONS: Read the passage. Then, choose or write the best answer.

How to Make a Terrarium

A terrarium is a miniature garden. It grows inside a covered glass or plastic container. A terrarium can easily be made out of common materials.

To make a terrarium, you first need to gather some supplies. You will need a 2-liter soda bottle, a marker, a sharp pair of scissors, 2 cups of soil, some seeds, a few rocks, and a spray bottle of water.

First, wash out the soda bottle and remove the label. Then, use the marker to draw a line around the bottle about $\frac{1}{3}$ of the way from the bottom. Use the sharp scissors to cut along the line so that the bottle is in two pieces. Be very careful doing this step!

After you have prepared the bottle, place the rocks in the bottom of the bottle. You can add peat moss, too. This will give the roots more room to breathe. Lightly pour the soil over the rocks and peat moss. Place the seeds in the soil. Follow the directions on the seed packet to know how deep to plant them.

Finally, lightly spray the soil with water. Slide the top of the bottle down over the bottom so that it overlaps. Keep the cap on. This will keep moisture in the bottle. Place your terrarium in the sun and watch your plants grow!

Your plants will grow nicely in the terrarium with very little work. If the soil starts to look dry, simply open the cap and spray in a little bit of water.

Strategy

As you read a how-to passage, find details that tell when each step is done and how. The order of steps connects ideas.

Test Tip

How-to passages tell how to do something. Look for words such as *first, next, then, last,* and *finally*.

1. **How are the paragraphs in this passage connected?**

   (A) cause and effect

   (B) sequence

   (C) compare and contrast

   (D) facts and details

2. **Look at your answer to the previous question. Why did the author choose to write the passage this way?**

   _____

   _____

   _____

3. **Which words does the author use to show how ideas are connected?**

   _____

   _____

4. **Why does the author tell you to keep the top on the bottle?**

   _____

   _____

5. **What is the purpose of putting rocks and peat moss under the soil?**

   (A) to make the level higher

   (B) to hold the roots in place

   (C) to look pretty

   (D) to give the roots room to breathe

6. **What would happen if the author didn't connect the sentences and paragraphs in this passage? Reread the passage and think about the information given.**

   _____

   _____

   _____

English Language Arts

Use Tools to Find Information
Reading: Informational Text

DIRECTIONS: Read the passage. Then, choose or write the best answer.

Gorillas

A gorilla is a <u>primate</u>. Gorillas live on the ground and are mostly <u>herbivores</u>. Gorillas live in the <u>forests</u> of Central Africa. Gorilla's <u>genes</u> are very similar to human genes.

Most gorillas live in <u>tropical forests</u>. Some gorillas, called <u>mountain gorillas</u>, live in the cloud forests of the <u>Virunga Volcanoes</u>. Other gorillas, called lowland gorillas, live in dense forests and <u>swamps</u>.

Gorilla Facts

Have longer arms than legs

Walk on their knuckles

Eat mostly leaves, stems, shrubs, and vines

Live about 35 years in the wild

Live in groups

Active in morning and late afternoon

Strategy Find information in a passage by using all the features presented, including underlined words, information in boxes, and visuals such as diagrams.

Test Tip A hyperlink is usually shown underlined and in blue. A hyperlink will take you to another page on the Internet that gives more information about the word.

1. **Which word can you click on to find out more about what gorillas eat?**

   (A) primate

   (B) herbivores

   (C) Africa

   (D) genes

2. **What would you do if you wanted to learn more about forests?**

   _____

   _____

3. **Where can you find more information about gorillas?**

   (A) rereading the passage

   (B) using a dictionary

   (C) reading the box with facts

   (D) clicking the word *Africa*

4. **What information is provided in the box but not in the passage?**

   _____

   _____

   _____

   _____

5. **What are different types of gorillas found in Africa?**

   _____

   _____

   _____

6. **How are all gorillas alike? Choose all that apply.**

   (A) They are primates.

   (B) They are mostly herbivores.

   (C) They live in cloud forests.

   (D) They live in swamps.

Use Tools to Find Information
Reading: Informational Text

DIRECTIONS: Read the passage. Then, choose or write the best answer.

Speedy Animals

What do you think is the fastest animal in the world? Animals use their speed to catch prey. Animals also use their speed to keep from becoming the prey of larger animals.

The cheetah is the fastest land animal. Cheetahs can reach top speeds of 113 kilometers per hour. This is about three times as fast as the fastest human runner! A cheetah can get up to 100 kilometers per hour in just three seconds. A cheetah uses its tail for more than just swatting flies. Cheetahs use their tails for steering while they run. The cheetah is the only big cat that can turn in mid-air while it is sprinting.

The fastest bird on earth is the Peregrine falcon. When the falcon is in a hunting dive, it can reach speeds up to 322 kilometers per hour! When it is just cruising, it can fly up to 90 kilometers per hour. The Peregrine falcon has amazing eyesight, making it the best hunter in its family. The falcon's eyes are bigger and heavier than human eyes. They can spot prey on the ground from 300 meters in the air.

The sailfish is the world's fastest fish. Sailfish have been clocked leaping out of the ocean at more than 110 kilometers per hour. Sailfish get their name from the fin on their backs. This fin runs down almost their entire body. The fin is taller than the thickness of the body. Sailfish eat sardines, anchovies, squid, and octopus.

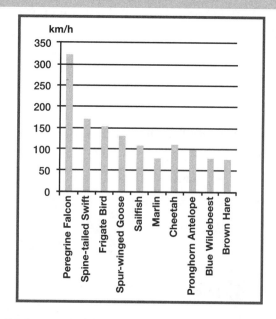

Strategy

Figure out how all of the information in a passage is connected by reading key words, information in sidebars, or looking at illustrations.

Test Tip

Graphs, diagrams, and charts give information in a visual way. Read these features carefully, looking at any labels or captions to make sure you understand what information is given.

1. What is the topic of the passage?

(A) the fastest animals on land

(B) the fastest bird in the world

(C) the fastest animals in the world

(D) the fastest fish in the ocean

2. Based on the topic, what kind of details should you look for in the passage that would support a main idea?

(A) names of animals

(B) speed of animals

(C) size of animals

(D) habitat of animals

3. Look at the graph. What information is given in the graph?

_____

4. How does the graph help you understand the passage?

(A) It shows how the animals' speeds compare.

(B) It shows the speeds of all the fast animals.

(C) It shows different animal speeds.

(D) It shows which animal is the fastest.

English Language Arts

Identify Point of View
Reading: Informational Text

DIRECTIONS: Choose or write the best answer.

> **School Uniforms**
> Students in Kenosha Schools should have to wear uniforms. Students who wear uniforms do better in school. There is less bullying because students are not teased about their clothes. Students can focus on schoolwork instead of on what everyone is wearing. School uniforms also save families money. Parents don't have to buy their children a lot of new school clothes every year. Parents can just buy a few uniforms for their children to wear.

Strategy   As you read, look for the author's point of view, or what he or she thinks, feels, or believes about the topic. Compare the author's point of view to your own.

Test Tip   Authors write passages to share their ideas and opinions on a topic. The author should include details that support their thoughts or opinions.

1. **What is the author's opinion?**

   _____

2. **Write two details that support the opinion you wrote above.**

   _____

   _____

3. **Which detail does NOT support the author's point of view?**

   (A) Students who wear uniforms do better in school.

   (B) School uniforms save families money.

   (C) School uniforms are usually boring.

   (D) School uniforms cut down on bullying.

4. **How can school uniforms help students focus on schoolwork?**

   _____

   _____

5. **Why does the author think that school uniforms cut down on bullying?**

   (A) Students can't tease each other about their clothes.

   (B) Students focus on their work and not on what others are wearing.

   (C) Parents can just buy a few uniforms.

   (D) Students don't need to buy a lot of new clothes each year.

6. **Do you agree or disagree with the author's point of view? Explain.**

   _____

   _____

   _____

   _____

   _____

   _____

Name _____ Date _____

Identify Point of View
Reading: Informational Text

DIRECTIONS: Read the passage. Then, choose or write the best answer.

> **A Winter Day**
> Ah, a winter's day is a beautiful gift! How I love the feel of light, fluffy snowflakes on my face, the brisk, chill air through my hair, and the bite of the cold on my nose. There is always plenty of play on a cold day, too. To run through the snow is a joy. To slide on the ice, a sweet dance. To fly down the hill on slippery snow and ice is a thrill! Such a day is never a waste. A time to be free, a time to play. Oh, the winter is joy, it is happiness. The snow, the cold, the clean air is a special gift!

Strategy   Identify the author's point of view by finding words that show feelings or thoughts about how they feel about a topic. Compare your feelings about the topic to the author's feelings.

Test Tip   Authors share facts about topics. Sometimes, authors also share what they think or how they feel about a topic.

1. **How does the author of the passage feel about winter?**

   (A) hates winter

   (B) loves winter

   (C) thinks winter is boring

   (D) wishes winter would end

2. **Write words that the author uses to show his or her feelings.**

   _____

   _____

3. **Why might the author have written this passage?**

   (A) to share ideas about winter activities

   (B) to give reasons to stay inside in the cold

   (C) to present an opinion about winter

   (D) to give facts about the seasons

4. **If a person who didn't like winter read this passage, how do you think they would feel about it? Explain your answer.**

   _____

   _____

5. **Would someone who loves summer like reading this passage? Explain.**

   _____

   _____

6. **Do you agree with the author? Explain your answer.**

   _____

   _____

English Language Arts

Compare and Contrast Texts
Reading: Informational Text

DIRECTIONS: Read each passage. Then, choose or write the best answer.

William Henry Harrison
by Helen Pawelski

You probably know that George Washington was our country's first president. You may also know that Abraham Lincoln was the president who ended slavery. But there are a lot more presidents that you probably have never heard of.

William Henry Harrison was our ninth president. Harrison was elected president in 1840 at the age of 67. At the time, he was the oldest man to ever be elected president. He was also the last U.S. president who had lived under British rule before the United States became its own country. William was born on February 9, 1773. His family was well known and had plenty of money. William's father, Benjamin, was one of the men who had signed the Declaration of Independence in 1776. In college, William studied medicine. Later, he changed careers and joined the army.

William Harrison started working in government in 1798. He held some very important jobs. From 1801–1813, William was the governor of the Indiana Territories. During the War of 1812, William led the army to defeat British and Indian forces. After the war, William moved to Ohio and continued to work for the government. In 1836, William ran for president and lost. He tried again in 1840. This time he won. Shortly after he moved into the White House, William caught a cold that turned into pneumonia. Before his wife had even moved to Washington, D.C. to be with him, William had died. William Henry Harrison had been president for only 32 days. Not only was he the shortest-serving president, he was the first president to die in office.

A Forgotten President
by Margaret Harms

Have you ever heard of William Henry Harrison? Even though he was the ninth president of the United States, he was the first for a lot of reasons. Harrison was not only the oldest president in office, but he also served for the shortest period of time.

William Henry Harrison was elected president of the United States in 1840. He was 67 years old. This was a big deal, because he was the oldest a president of the United States had ever been! It would be 140 years before another person replaced Harrison as the "oldest president."

Unfortunately, Harrison is not most famous for his age, but for his death. After 32 days in office, William Henry Harrison died of pneumonia. While this was upsetting, some good did come from it. No one had ever died in office before, so when Harrison did, it forced people to figure out what to do if this were to ever happen again.

Strategy

When reading two passages on the same topic, make a list of information that is in both passages and a list of information that is only in one of the passages. Use your lists to compare and contrast.

Test Tip

Keep in mind that each passage has its own main idea, even if the topic is the same. The details may be similar, but they support different main ideas.

1. **What is the main idea of "William Henry Harrison"?**

   (A) Harrison was the bravest president.

   (B) Harrison was the most popular president.

   (C) Harrison was a president that most don't know.

   (D) Harrison was the first to die from pneumonia.

English Language Arts

Compare and Contrast Texts
Reading: Informational Texts

DIRECTIONS: Choose or write the best answer.

> **Strategy** | Identify the main idea of each passage by using the facts, ideas, or opinions that the authors share in each passage.

> **Test Tip** | Different passages on the same topic will have details that are unique, or details that one passage has that the other does not have.

2. **What is the main idea of "A Forgotten President"?**

   (A) Harrison was should not have been president.

   (B) Harrison had a lot of firsts in his presidency.

   (C) Harrison set a record that was never broken.

   (D) Harrison was seriously ill but still elected.

3. **Compare the two passages. What do these two passages have in common?**

   _____

   _____

4. **Reread each passage. What information is given in the first passage that is not included in the second passage?**

   _____

   _____

5. **Use details from the first passage to put the events that led to Harrison's presidency in order. Write the numbers 2, 3, 4, and 5.**

   [1] Harrison went to medical school.

   [ ] Harrison lost the election in 1836.

   [ ] Harrison was the governor for the Indiana territories.

   [ ] Harrison joined the army.

   [ ] Harrison led the army to defeat British and Indian forces.

6. **What information is given in the second passage that is not included in the first passage?**

   _____

   _____

   _____

   _____

7. **Why does the author of the second passage call Harrison's death "good"?**

   _____

   _____

   _____

   _____

   Write the key detail that helped you answer the question above.

   _____

   _____

   _____

   _____

English Language Arts

Compare and Contrast Texts
Reading: Informational Texts

DIRECTIONS: Read each passage.

Moths and Butterflies
by Jennifer Eastin

Moths and butterflies are similar in many ways. Moths and butterflies both start as larvae. The larvae are caterpillars. Moth and butterfly caterpillars are both long and soft. Sometimes, they have protective spikes or hairs on their bodies. They both have heads with mouths for eating. Caterpillars have six pairs of jointed legs. They also have 1 to 5 pairs of soft, unjointed legs. Most caterpillars are green or brown. They have color patterns for camouflage. Some caterpillars are poisonous. They have bright colors to warn predators that they are deadly.

Adult moths and butterflies have large wings covered in scales. Each scale is a different color. This is what gives them their beautiful patterns. Moths and butterflies are the only insects that have these scales on their wings. Butterflies usually hold their wings up over their backs. Moths, on the other hand, fold their wings under their bodies. Like caterpillars, adult moths and butterflies have colors that either camouflage them or warn predators of their danger.

Moths and butterflies have special mouthparts for sucking. These mouthparts coil up into a spiral. No other insect has a mouthpart like this. The bodies of adult moths and butterflies are soft and covered with fine hairs. Butterflies and moths both have large eyes and a set of antennae. Butterfly antennae are thin with a thick part at the top. Moth antennae are thin all the way to the tip. Some moths have antennae with side branches that look like feathers.

Winged Wonders
by Lynn Weinstein

Moths and butterflies may be different insects, but they are quite similar. Both of these insects start out as caterpillars. The caterpillars have long, soft bodies. Sometimes, the bodies are covered with hair or spikes to protect against danger. Moth and butterfly caterpillars are usually green or brown. This allows them to blend into their environment and protects them from predators. Some caterpillars are poisonous. To warn predators, these caterpillars are brightly colored. Predators know not to eat them.

When caterpillars come out of their cocoons, they are adult butterflies or moths. Butterflies and moths have many things in common. Both have large wings. Their wings are covered with scales. Each scale adds a different color to the beautiful wing patterns you see. Butterflies hold their wings up and behind their bodies. Moths usually fold their wings underneath their bodies. The colors on the wings of moths and butterflies serve the same purpose as the colors of a caterpillar. Green and brown colors allow them to hide from predators. Bright colors warn predators to stay away.

Adult moths and butterflies have a special mouth that no other insect has. Their mouth is shaped like a straw and coils up into a spiral. Butterflies and moths have large eyes. They also have antennae. Butterfly and moth antennae look different. Butterfly antennae have a thick part at the end. Moths' antennae are usually thin all the way to the tip. Sometimes, moth antennae have little branches that look like feathers.

English Language Arts

Compare and Contrast Texts
Reading: Informational Texts

DIRECTIONS: Use the passages to choose or write the best answer.

Strategy | As you read two passages on the same topic, determine how the main idea of each passage is similar and different. Use the most important ideas and details to identify the main idea of each passage.

Test Tip | Comparing and contrasting is easier to do if you organize your ideas. Make a chart to list details that are the same and details that are different.

1. **What is the main idea of both passages?**

   (A) Butterflies and moths are different insects.

   (B) Butterflies and moths are similar in many ways.

   (C) Butterflies and moths both start their lives as caterpillars.

   (D) Butterflies are prettier than moths.

2. **Why do some butterflies and moths have brightly colored wings?**

   _____

   _____

3. **Reread each passage. Write one key detail from each passage about how butterflies and moths protect themselves.**

   _____

   _____

   _____

   _____

   _____

   _____

4. **Are the details you wrote for #3 important? How do the details support the main idea?**

   _____

   _____

   _____

   _____

   _____

   _____

5. **Write a key detail that tells how moths and butterflies are different from other insects.**

   _____

   _____

   _____

6. **Write two key details about how moths and butterflies are different.**

   _____

   _____

   _____

   _____

English Language Arts

Determine the Meaning of Words and Phrases
Language

DIRECTIONS: Choose or write the best answer.

Strategy — To determine the meaning of an unknown word, look at the words and phrases around the unknown word. These are clues to the meaning.

Test Tip — Think about the meaning of the sentence as a whole. Then, choose the meaning that fits with the sentence.

1. Anna used the garden _____ to wash the dog.

   (A) rake
   (B) seeds
   (C) hose
   (D) gate

   All of these words are objects used in a garden. Write how you chose the correct answer.

   _____

   _____

2. The thrilling ride on the roller coaster made us yell loudly.

   Choose two words that mean the same as thrilling.

   (A) exciting
   (B) boring
   (C) slow
   (D) awesome

3. Write a word to complete this sentence.

   The _____ weather will continue all night, but we will be safe and sound inside.

   _____

   What context clues helped you write your answer?

   _____

4. Before Samantha awoke, I left her present beside her bed.

   What does the word awoke mean?

   _____

   How did looking at the parts of the word awoke help you determine its meaning?

   _____

   _____

5. Sam's grades have really improved. He had a C at the beginning of the year, and now he has an A.

   What does improved mean?

   (A) gotten better
   (B) gotten worse
   (C) fixed
   (D) dropped

6. Sarah is being very disagreeable today.

   What does the word disagreeable mean?

   _____

   _____

Name _____ Date _____

English Language Arts

Determine the Meaning of Words and Phrases
Language

DIRECTIONS: Choose or write the best answer.

Strategy To determine the meaning of an unknown word, look at the parts of a word that you know, such as prefixes and suffixes.

7. Explain how knowing that the prefix *un-* means "not" can help you find the meaning of the word *unable.*

_____

_____

8. Which word part can help you find the meaning of the word *fearless*?

_____

_____

9. For each word, write the prefix, root, and suffix.

Word	Prefix	Root	Suffix
incompletion			
disappearance			
unreasonable			
reusable			

DIRECTIONS: Use the prefixes and suffixes below to answer questions 10–11.

Prefix/Meaning	Suffix/Meaning
in	-less "without"
re- "again"	-able "able to"
un- "not"	-ful "having, full of"

Test Tip

Find the root word and use its meaning to figure out the meaning of an unknown word.

10. Use the root word *help* and a prefix to make a word that means "without help."

_____

Write how you know.

_____

_____

Write a sentence using your word.

_____

_____

11. Which word means "not able to be stopped"?

Ⓐ disstop

Ⓑ unstop

Ⓒ stoppable

Ⓓ unstoppable

Write how you know.

_____

_____

English Language Arts

Understand Word Relationships and Nuances

Language

DIRECTIONS: Choose or write the best answer.

Rita was watching a television show about jellyfish. She thought she knew that she would know much of the information that was being given, because she lived near the ocean and had seen jellyfish many times. During the program, she learned several new facts about jellyfish. After the program, she wanted learn more about jellyfish. She took steps to find out more. First, she went online. She did a search for jellyfish. She found some more information that she hadn't known before. She thought if it was all true.

Strategy

As you read sentences, use synonyms and antonyms of words to find the exact meaning.

Test Tip

There are often several words that mean the same thing, such as *yell, shout, scream,* and *bellow*. All of these words are about speaking loudly. But each word has a slightly different meaning. For example, you might scream in fear, but not bellow.

1. **What word would be better in sentence 2 than thought she knew?**

   (A) suspected
   (B) wondered
   (C) knew
   (D) heard

   Write how you know.

   _____

   _____

   _____

2. **The story says that Rita took steps to learn more about jellyfish. Explain what this means in the context of the story.**

   _____

   _____

   _____

3. **What would be a better word for thought in the last sentence?**

   (A) suspected
   (B) discovered
   (C) learned
   (D) wondered

   Write how you know.

   _____

   _____

   _____

4. **Jacob was pulling at his mother's hand. He was very impatient and wanted to get to the park. His mother was on the phone and told Jimmy, "Hold your horses! We'll go in a few minutes."**

   What does impatient mean?

   _____

   _____

English Language Arts

Understand Word Relationships and Nuances
Language

DIRECTIONS: Choose or write the best answer.

Strategy Try out different meanings in the sentence to find the correct one.

Test Tip Remember that nonliteral words and phrases mean something other than the dictionary definition. Use the sentence to determine meaning.

5. **Which two sentences use the word *trim* in the same way?**

   (A) We will trim the Christmas tree on December 15.

   (B) I went to the barber shop to get a trim.

   (C) Dad really needs to trim those bushes!

   (D) Mom likes to trim the turkey with stuffing and cranberries.

   Write how you know.

   _____

   _____

6. **Five-year-old Austin was <u>bouncing off the walls</u> because he was going to see the circus for the very first time.**

   What does the underlined phrase mean?

   _____

   _____

7. **Which of the words below fit in the category of "helpful"? Choose all that apply.**

   (A) doctors

   (B) wheelchairs

   (C) lab coats

   (D) firefighters

8. **Isaac was very angry about losing his baseball glove. He was yelling and screaming. His friend told him that he needed to get a grip. Isaac grabbed onto the railing and wouldn't let go.**

   What did Isaac's friend really mean?

   _____

   _____

   Why is Isaac's response funny?

   _____

   _____

9. **Which list would you use for the words *thunder, drums, siren*?**

   (A) blaring or piercing

   (B) storms or weather

   (C) musical or singing

   (D) playing or learning

10. **Write three words that fit with the word *colorful*. Words can be nouns or verbs.**

    _____

    _____

    Write how you know.

    _____

    _____

English Language Arts

Write an Opinion
Writing

DIRECTIONS: An opinion paragraph tells what you think or how you feel about a topic. It gives reasons why you think or feel that way. Write an opinion paragraph for the school newspaper about a book that everyone in your class should read. Your paragraph should have:

- A sentence to introduce your topic

- A statement of your opinion

- An organizational structure

- Reasons to support your opinion

- Linking words and phrases to connect your opinion and reasons

- A sentence to end your paragraph

Strategy

Plan your writing by stating your opinion and listing reasons you have that opinion. Then, begin writing. When you are finished writing, read your paragraph to yourself. Make sure you included everything listed in the directions. Make sure your writing is clear and fix any errors.

Test Tip

An opinion must be supported with reasons. Reasons tell why you think or feel a certain way. Include details from the book that support your reasons.

Everyone should read the book:
Reason 1:
Details:
Reason 2:
Details:
Reason 3:
Details:
Conclusion:

English Language Arts

Write an Opinion
Writing

DIRECTIONS: Write your paragraph on the lines. Use the checklist to make sure your paragraph has all of the parts needed.

Test Tip   Use your graphic organizer as you write to keep your ideas organized and so you don't forget to include an idea or detail.

Checklist

☐ I introduced my topic.

☐ I stated my opinion.

☐ I gave at least two reasons for my opinion.

☐ I supported my reasons with details.

☐ I used linking words.

☐ I have a good conclusion.

☐ My sentences all make sense.

☐ I used nouns and verbs correctly.

☐ I used capital letters properly.

☐ I used correct punctuation.

☐ I spelled all of my words correctly.

_____

_____

_____

_____

_____

_____

_____

_____

_____

_____

English Language Arts

Write an Informative Text
Writing

DIRECTIONS: An informative text gives facts and details about a topic. Write an informative text about a pet or an animal that you know a lot about. Your paragraph should have:

- A sentence to introduce your topic

- Facts about your subject

- Definitions and details about your subject

- Linking words and phrases to connect your ideas

- A sentence to end your paragraph

Strategy

Plan your writing by listing details that relate to your topic or facts. Then, begin writing. When you are finished writing, read your paragraph to yourself. Make sure you included everything listed in the directions. Make sure your writing is clear and fix any errors.

Test Tip

Facts are information that is true. Informative pieces can give opinions, but they mostly give facts about a topic. Try to think of at least two details for each fact.

Topic:
Fact 1:
Details:
Fact 2:
Details:
Fact 3:
Details:
Conclusion:

English Language Arts

Write an Informative Text
Writing

DIRECTIONS: Write your paragraph on the lines. Use the checklist to make sure your paragraph has the information needed.

Test Tip Use the graphic organizer with your facts and details to write your informational text. Be sure to connect ideas with linking words.

Checklist

- ☐ I introduced my topic.
- ☐ I gave at least two facts about my topic.
- ☐ I supported my facts with details.
- ☐ I used linking words.
- ☐ I have a good conclusion.
- ☐ My sentences all make sense.
- ☐ I used nouns and verbs correctly.
- ☐ I used capital letters properly.
- ☐ I used correct punctuation.
- ☐ I spelled all of my words correctly.

English Language Arts

Write a Narrative
Writing

DIRECTIONS: A narrative is a story that tells about real or imagined events. Write a narrative about a fun experience you have had. Your paragraph should have:

- A narrator and/or characters

- A natural sequence of events

- Dialogue

- Descriptions of actions, thoughts, and feelings

- Time words and phrases to show the order of events

- A sentence to end your paragraph

Strategy Plan a narrative by choosing people, places, and events that will be in the story. Remember that a story should have a beginning, middle, and end.

Test Tip Include details that help your readers understand the event and imagine it in their minds.

Experience:
Event 1:
Details:
Event 2:
Details:
Event 3:
Details:
Conclusion:

English Language Arts

Write a Narrative
Writing

DIRECTIONS: Write your paragraph on the lines. Use the checklist to make sure your paragraph has everything.

Test Tip | Use your organizer as you write your narrative to make sure events are in order and that you use details.

Checklist

☐ I introduced my narrator and/or characters.

☐ I explained the problem in the story.

☐ I wrote a clear sequence of events that happened.

☐ I used dialogue and wrote about the characters' actions, thoughts, and feelings.

☐ I used time words.

☐ I have a good conclusion.

☐ My sentences all make sense.

☐ I used nouns and verbs correctly.

☐ I used capital letters properly.

☐ I used correct punctuation.

☐ I spelled all of my words correctly.

English Language Arts

Understand Editing and Revising
Writing

DIRECTIONS: Read the paragraph. Underline places in the paragraph that are not clear. Then, rewrite the paragraph on the lines so it makes sense.

Strategy — Revise to make sure your writing makes sense. Then, edit to fix errors. Use what you know about nouns, verbs, adjectives, and adverbs to make correct choices when you edit.

Test Tip — When you are revising a paragraph, read it out loud to yourself. Listen for anything that does not sound right or does not make sense.

Last summer, I went on vacation with my family. We drove across the country. First, we stopped in Sioux Falls. It is in South Dakota. It is very pretty there. We saw the waterfall. The city is named after it. It was very cool. Then, we left and went somewhere else. It was farther west. It was called the Badlands. It is called that because the land is very dry and things can't grow well. We went on a helicopter ride. It was so cool! After South Dakota, we went to Wyoming to see Devil's Tower because my dad really likes *Close Encounters of the Third Kind* and that is where it was made and we went to Colorado. We went rafting and my brother jumped off a big rock. The water was really cold. It was fun when we took the train to the top of Pike's Peak. Then, we drove home. It was a long vacation. It was two weeks. We had a lot of fun.

_____

_____

_____

_____

_____

_____

_____

_____

_____

_____

_____

_____

Understand Editing and Revising
Writing

DIRECTIONS: Read the paragraph. Look for spelling, capitalization, and punctuation mistakes. Rewrite the paragraph correctly on the lines.

Strategy   Reread your writing out loud to find punctuation mistakes. To find spelling and capitalization errors, try reading backward, looking at each word.

    Last week my family went to an amusement park for the day we went on a lot of rides. My favrit ride was a roller coaster call the demon. The demon goes upside down for times. I was scared at first but my mom went with me and she had gone on it many times since she was my age. Wen we were done on the demon we went on the bumper cars the swings and the log ride. I like to go to the amusement park on wednesday becuz there are not a lot of people and the lines are shortest. Next time we go to the amusement park I want to go on another roller coaster. They are so much fun!

_____
_____
_____
_____
_____
_____
_____
_____
_____
_____
_____
_____
_____
_____

Strategy Review

In this section, you will review the strategies you learned and apply them to practice the skills.

Strategy

Use details from a story or passage to show your understanding.

When you read a story, think about how a character's thoughts, words, and actions show how he or she is feeling.

EXAMPLE

Read the story carefully. Then, answer the questions using details from the story.

Juan looked at the clock. He paced across the floor. His best friend, Bill, was coming to visit for the first time in six months. Bill had moved very far away. Juan wondered if they would still feel like good friends.

The doorbell rang, and Juan raced to answer it. Bill looked a bit unsure. Juan smiled and started talking just as he always had when they had lived near one another. He made Bill feel comfortable. As the day went on, it felt like old times.

How do Juan's actions show that he was nervous and excited? Think about how someone might act if he were nervous or excited. Look back at how the author describes Juan's actions. "Juan looked at the clock. He paced across the floor." This is something a person who is excited or nervous would do.

1. **Why was Juan so excited about his friend coming over?**

_____

2. **How did Juan try to make Bill feel comfortable?**

_____

How did the strategy help you answer these questions?

_____

_____

Strategy

Make a picture in your mind as you read.

Read the story. Then, answer the questions.

One day in the times when the sky was close to the ground, a woman went out to pound rice. Before she began her work, she took off the beads from around her neck and the comb from her hair. She hung the comb and beads in the sky. Then, she began working. Each time she raised her pestle into the air to pound the rice, it hit the sky. The sky began to rise. It went up so far that the woman lost her beads and comb. Never did they come back down, for the comb became the moon and the beads became the stars that are scattered about.

As you read this story, picture a woman kneeling in the sand, with a bowl in front of her. Imagine her take the beads from around her neck and the comb out of her hair and hang them above her head.

3. **What else do you see in your mind when you read this story?**

_____

_____

4. **Based on the story, what do you think a *pestle* is?**

Ⓐ a tool for mashing food

Ⓑ a trinket for holding hair away from the face

Ⓒ a bowl for holding rice

Ⓓ a piece of jewelry

Which words helped you determine the meaning?

_____

_____

Strategy Review

Strategy
Reread to answer questions.

EXAMPLE
Read the story carefully. Then, answer the questions.

One day, Margaret went for a walk at the lakefront. She listened to some music as she walked. A little way down the path, Margaret noticed something shining in the water. She peered at it for a long time before she could make it out. It was silvery and round. Margaret took out her phone and snapped a picture. When she looked at the picture, she noticed that there were tiny windows along the middle of the object. Margaret found a shady spot at the edge of the lake and watched the silvery object. It seemed to be vibrating. Suddenly, the water around the object began to move. The silver object lifted slowly from the surface of the lake. It hovered for a moment and then zipped away. Margaret reached for her phone to take a picture, but before her fingers even touched her phone, the object was gone.

Reread to find details.
Describe what Margaret saw in the water.
Make sure to use details from the story. Reread to find a description of what Margaret saw. The story says, "It was silvery and round."

1. **Why did Margaret go to the edge of the lake?**
   - (A) She was tired from walking.
   - (B) She wanted to listen to music.
   - (C) She wanted to watch the object in the water.
   - (D) She was texting her friend.

2. **What did Margaret see when she looked at the picture of the object on her phone?**

   _____

   _____

Strategy
Ask questions as you read.

Read the passage carefully. Then, answer the questions.

A timpani is a large drum with a stretchable head and a pedal that can be used to change the pitch of the drum. This makes it different from other drums. The pitch of other drums cannot be changed. The smallest timpani is 26 inches around, while the largest is 32 inches around. Timpani evolved from military drums.

As you read, ask questions to make sure you understand the story or passage. You can ask questions such as *Who is in the story? What is the passage mainly about? What happens in the story? What information is given?* Then, reread the story or passage to find answers.

3. **What is the name of a large drum that has a pedal to change the pitch?**
   - (A) drum
   - (B) timpani
   - (C) stretchable
   - (D) military

   What question can you ask yourself to find the answer?

   _____

   _____

4. **How is a timpani different from other drums?**

   _____

   _____

English Language Arts

Strategy Review

Strategy
Pay attention to how parts of a story or passage connect and fit together.

EXAMPLE

Read the passage carefully. Then, answer the questions.

A firefly is a soft-bodied beetle that is related to the glowworm. The male firefly can fly, but the female cannot. A firefly's light is caused by a chemical reaction. The firefly can control this. This means that the firefly can control when the light turns on and off. Young fireflies use their lights as a defense against predators. Adult fireflies use their light patterns to identify others of their type.

Look for words that show connections.
Certain key words can help you understand the passage. In the sentence, "The male firefly can fly, but the female cannot," the word but tells you that the author is contrasting two things. In the sentence, "A firefly's light is caused by a chemical reaction," the words is caused by tell you that there is a cause and effect relationship.

1. **Why aren't fireflies always using their lights?**

   _____

   _____

2. **What causes a firefly's light?**
   (A) predators
   (B) a chemical reaction
   (C) the sun
   (D) batteries

   Write the words that show the connection for this idea.

   _____

Strategy
Plan your writing using a graphic organizer.

Before you start writing, make a plan of what you are going to include. Use a numbered list or other graphic organizer to keep your ideas in order.

EXAMPLE

Write a story about going to a birthday party.

Who: my sister and I
What: my friend's birthday party
When: last Saturday
Where: a pizza place

Details:
First: cheese pizza
Second: games
Third: chocolate cake
Fourth: opened gifts

3. **Use transition words to plan a story about a trip to the zoo.**

   Who: _____
   What: _____
   When: _____
   Where: _____

   Details:
   First: _____
   Second: _____
   Third: _____
   Fourth: _____

Strategy Review

Strategy   When you write, use details to support main ideas.

EXAMPLE
Use the plan you made to guide your writing.

    Last week was my friend Sadie's birthday. She invited my sister and me to her birthday party. It was at a pizza restaurant. When we got there, the pizza was already on the tables. I ate three slices of cheese pizza. After pizza, Sadie's mom gave us all tokens to play games. We played for a whole hour! I won 142 tickets and traded them in for a stuffed animal. After games, we sang, "Happy Birthday" to Sadie and ate chocolate cake. Finally, Sadie opened her presents. She opened mine last. I had given her a copy of my favorite book. She loved it!

Write a story about a trip to the zoo using the plan you created on page 53.

_____

_____

_____

_____

_____

_____

Strategy   Revise to make sure your writing makes sense. Then, edit to fix errors. Use what you know about nouns, verbs, adjectives, and adverbs to make correct choices when you edit.

Look for words that need capital letters.
Look for places that need punctuation.
Read the sentences carefully to see if they make sense.

Is the best buy store opin at 8 oclock!
mary said i like ice cream more than popsicles
witch hazel elementary school is the best school around?

Rewrite the sentences on the lines so that they are correct.

1. _____

2. _____

3. _____

Strategies for Mathematics Tests

Read the strategies below to learn more about how they work.

Use basic operations to solve problems.

You can use what you know about adding, subtracting, multiplying, and dividing to solve many different types of problems. Make sure you know your basic math facts. This will save time on the test and ensure your answers are correct.

Use graphs, tables, and drawings to understand data.

Sometimes, making a drawing of a word problem helps you figure out how to solve it. Other times, making a graph or line plot is a way to show numbers or amounts of something. Drawings, number lines, line plots, and other graphs all use numbers.

Read word problems carefully. Make sure you know what you are asked to do.

Whenever you need to solve a word problem, you should first ask *What information do I know?* Then, you should ask *What question am I being asked to answer?* or *What am I being asked to find?* Don't start solving until you know the answers to these questions!

Choose the right tool and units to measure objects.

Certain tools are used to measure length, weight, and temperature. Remember that measurements all have units. Lengths are often measured in inches (in.), feet (ft.), centimeters (cm), or meters (m). Weight is often measured in pounds (lb.), grams (g), or kilograms (kg). Temperature can be measured in degrees Celsius (°C) or degrees Fahrenheit (°F).

Use what you know about numbers, shapes, and measurement to answer questions.

Using what you already know about numbers, shapes, and measurement, you can answer many different types of questions.

Interpret Products of Whole Numbers
Operations and Algebraic Thinking

DIRECTIONS: Choose or write the correct answer.

Strategy Use multiplication to solve many types of problems.

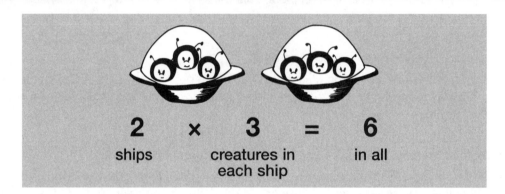

2 × **3** = **6**
ships   creatures in   in all
each ship

1. Mikala is having a party. She sets up the tables and chairs as shown below. Which multiplication sentence shows how to find the total number of chairs?

 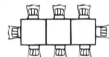 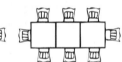

   (A) 6 × 4 = 24
   (B) 3 × 3 = 9
   (C) 3 × 9 = 27
   (D) 3 × 8 = 24

2. Write a multiplication sentence that you can use to find the total number of black triangles in the picture below.

_____

Test Tip

Remember, there are 7 days in one week.

3. Emile will practice baseball every day for 7 weeks. How many days will Emile practice baseball? Show your work.

_____

4. Which two are the same as 5 × 8?

   (A) 5 × 8 × 5 × 8 × 5 × 8
   (B) 8 × 8 × 8 × 8 × 8
   (C) 5 + 5 + 5 + 5 + 5 + 5 + 5 + 5
   (D) 8 + 8 + 8 + 8 + 8

Interpret Products of Whole Numbers
Operations and Algebraic Thinking

DIRECTIONS: Choose or write the correct answer.

Strategy | Make connections between pictures and numbers. Pictures of a multiplication number sentence often show equal groups of objects.

5. Which picture shows the multiplication of 2 × 4?

A

B

C

D

Test Tip

When more than one answer may be correct, read all choices first before choosing.

6. Jason is cutting out triangle shapes in the squares below to make a design. Which number sentence shows how many triangle shapes he will have? Choose all that apply.

(A) 5 × 8 = 40
(B) 8 × 8 = 64
(C) 8 × 5 = 40
(D) 5 × 4 = 20

7. Mrs. Sanchez is planting spring flowers in her garden. She has 8 packs of flowers with 6 flowers in each pack. What is the total number of flowers that Mrs. Sanchez plants? Use words, numbers, or pictures to show how you found the answer.

Interpret Quotients of Whole Numbers
Operations and Algebraic Thinking

DIRECTIONS: Choose or write the correct answer.

> **Strategy** — Use number sentences and pictures to solve problems involving division. Pictures of division often show a set of objects separated into equal groups.

EXAMPLE:

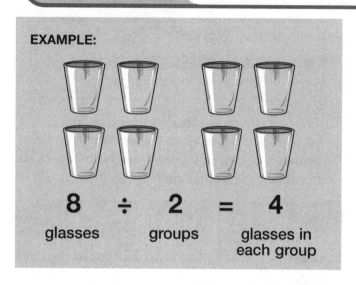

8 ÷ 2 = 4

glasses ÷ groups = glasses in each group

2. Meg and Myra gathered seashells in 4 buckets. They found 32 shells and put an equal number of shells in each bucket. Draw a picture of equal groups to find how many shells they put in each bucket.

1. There are 18 frogs in the pond. There are 2 frogs on each lily pad. How many lily pads have frogs on them? Use words, numbers, or pictures to show your answer.

3. Write a division number sentence for question 3 to show how many shells Meg and Myra put in each bucket.

_____

Interpret Quotients of Whole Numbers
Operations and Algebraic Thinking

Strategy To solve a division problem, find the unknown number of groups or the unknown group size.

4. Which picture shows the division of 12 ÷ 3?

Ⓐ

Ⓑ

Ⓒ

Ⓓ

5. There are 28 students in a class. If they break up into 4 equal teams, which number sentence shows how many students will be on each team?

Ⓐ 28 − 4 = 24

Ⓑ 28 ÷ 4 = 7

Ⓒ 28 + 4 = 32

Ⓓ 28 × 4 = 112

6. Write a word problem that can be solved using this number sentence. Then, solve it. Show your work.

$$54 ÷ 9 = \square$$

7. Write a division number sentence that is shown in this picture.

_____

Test Tip

Remember, the first number in a division number sentence represents the total number of objects divided into equal-sized groups.

Solve Problems: Multiply and Divide
Operations and Algebraic Thinking

DIRECTIONS: Choose or write the correct answer.

Strategy

As you read word problems, identify the numbers you will use to solve the problem. Then, identify the operations you need to use. Use this information to write a number sentence or draw a picture that helps you solve the problem.

EXAMPLE

A roller coaster holds a total of 54 people. Each car holds 6 people. Write and solve a number sentence that can be used to find how many cars are on the roller coaster. Use the letter c to stand for the numbers of cars.

$54 \div 6 = c$

$c = 9$

There are 9 cars on the roller coaster.

Test Tip

Remember, an array is an arrangement of objects, pictures, or numbers in columns and rows.

1. **There are 32 chairs in the classroom. The teacher is arranging them in rows with 8 chairs in each row.**

   Draw an array to show how many rows of chairs there will be.

2. **Write a number sentence for the problem in question 1.**

DIRECTIONS: Use the information below to help you answer questions 3 and 4.

You have a bag of 28 orange slices to share with some friends. You want each friend to get 7 slices.

3. **Which operation can you use to find how many friends you can share the orange slices with? Choose all that apply.**

   (A) Addition

   (B) Subtraction

   (C) Multiplication

   (D) Division

4. **Show how you can use one of the operations you chose to find the answer.**

5. **A package of socks contains 6 pairs. Write and solve a number sentence that can be used to find how many pairs are in 15 packages. Use the letter s to stand for the numbers of pairs of socks. Then, solve the number sentence. Show your work.**

Solve Problems: Multiply and Divide
Operations and Algebraic Thinking

DIRECTIONS: Choose or write the correct answer.

> **Strategy** Learn and remember common measurements so that you can use them in multiplication and division problems.

6. A square has 4 equal sides. How many sides do 9 squares have all together?

Ⓐ 13
Ⓑ 27
Ⓒ 36
Ⓓ 45

> **Test Tip**
>
> Remember, there are 36 inches in one yard.

7. Kylie has a piece of ribbon that is 1 yard long. She wants to cut it into 6 equal-sized pieces. How many inches long will each piece of ribbon be? Show your work.

DIRECTIONS: Use the information below to answer questions 9 and 10.

A park ranger sees 5 rabbits running into the woods.

9. Which number sentence shows many legs the park ranger sees?

Ⓐ 5 × 4 = ☐
Ⓑ 5 × 5= ☐
Ⓒ 5 + 4 = ☐
Ⓓ 5 + 5 + 5 = ☐

10. How many legs did the park ranger see?

_____

8. Jamie has some pencils shown below. He wants to put the same number of pencils in each of two boxes. How many pencils will be in each box?

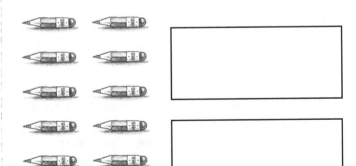

Determine Unknown Numbers
in Multiplication and Division Equations
Operations and Algebraic Thinking

DIRECTIONS: Choose or write the correct answer.

Strategy Use basic multiplication and division facts to find the value of an unknown number in a number sentence.

EXAMPLE:

Which number makes the equation true?

$5 \div 9 = ?$

9 groups of _____ make 54.

9 groups of 6 make 54.

So, $54 \div 9 = 6$

Test Tip

When an unknown number follows a multiplication sign, you need to find the missing factor.

1. **Which number makes the equation true?**

   $8 \times ? = 56$

   (A) 9
   (B) 8
   (C) 7
   (D) 6

2. **Matt has 6 cans of tennis balls. There are 3 tennis balls in each can. Write a multiplication equation to find the total tennis balls. Use a square ▢ to stand for the total number of tennis balls. Then, solve the number equation.**

   _____

   _____

3. **Leslie has a total of 40 flowers. She has 5 vases. The equation below shows the problem.**

   $40 \div ? = 5$

   How many flowers can Leslie put in each vase? Show your work.

4. **The number 6 makes which number sentence true? Choose all that apply.**

   (A) $? \times 8 = 48$
   (B) $6 \times ? = 36$
   (C) $48 \div ? = 7$
   (D) $? = 30 \div 5$

5. **Miss Nelson has 28 students in her class. They line up in 4 equal lines. Which equation shows how many students are in each line?**

   (A) $28 \times ▢ = 7$
   (B) $? \times 28 = ▢$
   (C) $28 \div 4 = 7$
   (D) $▢ \div 28 = 7$

6. **Soren has 8 packs of trading cards. There are 9 trading cards in each pack. Write a multiplication equation to find the total number of trading cards. Use a square ▢ to stand for the total number of trading cards. Then, solve the number equation.**

   _____

   _____

Math

Determine Unknown Numbers
in Multiplication and Division Equations
Operations and Algebraic Thinking

DIRECTIONS: Choose or write the correct answer.

Strategy To determine the unknown number in a division number sentence, think of a related multiplication fact.

7. Luis has 9 packs of pencils. Each pack contains 5 pencils. Write a number sentence to find how many pencils he has all together.

_____

8. Write a word problem that can be solved using the equation below. Then, solve it. Show your work.

$72 \div 8 = \square$

9. Ava played in three basketball games. In each of the first two games, she scored 9 points. In the third game, she scored 3 times as many points as in her first two games. Write and solve a number sentence to find how many points she scored in game 3.

_____

10. Tamara helps her dad put in a new kitchen floor. She carries 4 boxes of tiles into the kitchen. Each box holds 12 tiles. Which number sentence can be used to show the total number of tiles Tamara carries into the kitchen? Choose all that apply.

(A) $\square = 4 \times 12$

(B) $12 - 4 = \square$

(C) $48 \div 8 = \square$

(D) $\square \div 4 = 12$

11. Charlie arranged his book collection of 80 books on 4 shelves. He placed an equal number of books on each shelf. Write and solve a number sentence to find how many books were on each shelf.

_____

Apply Properties of Operations to Multiply and Divide

Operations and Algebraic Thinking

DIRECTIONS: Choose or write the correct answer.

Strategy Apply multiplication properties to find products. Multiply numbers in any order and any grouping. Use the rules for what happens when a number is multiplied by 0 or 1.

EXAMPLE

The order of numbers does not matter when you multiply.

$6 \times 5 = 5 \times 6$

$30 = 30$

The product stays the same when you change the grouping of the numbers.

$(2 \times 5) \times 6 = 2 \times (5 \times 6)$

$10 \times 6 = 2 \times 30$

$60 = 60$

DIRECTIONS: Write *true* or *false* for questions 1–4.

1. $4 \times 8 = 8 \times 4$ _____

2. $7 \times (4 \times 3) = (7 \times 4) \times 3$ _____

3. $9 \times 8 = 9 \times 9$ _____

4. $(2 \times 6) \times 1 = (1 \times 6) \times 2$ _____

5. Without multiplying, Alvina says that $3 \times 4 \times 2$ has the same product as $2 \times 4 \times 3$. Is Alvina correct? Show your work.

_____

_____

Test Tip

Remember the relationship between multiplication and division. One operation can undo the other.

6. Which two number sentences are BOTH correct?

(A) $6 \div 1 = 6$ and $1 \div 6 = 6$

(B) $6 \times 1 = 6$ and $6 \div 6 = 1$

(C) $6 \div 1 = 6$ and $6 \div 6 = 6$

(D) $6 \times 6 = 6$ and $6 \div 1 = 6$

7. Max says he can multiply the number 114,567 by 0 and get the answer immediately. How can he do that?

_____

_____

_____

DIRECTIONS: Use the information that follows to answer questions 8 and 9.

8. Mr. Thompson buys some cases of apples for his store. Each case of apples holds 4 bags of apples. Each bag holds 8 apples. Mr. Thompson buys 2 cases of apples. Which number sentence shows how many apples Mr. Thompson buys? Choose all that apply.

(A) $2 \times 4 \times 8 = \square$

(B) $8 \times 8 = \square$

(C) $2 \times 12 = \square$

(D) $4 \times 8 \times 2 = \square$

9. How many apples did Mr. Thompson buy?

_____

Apply Properties of Operations
to Multiply and Divide
Operations and Algebraic Thinking

DIRECTIONS: Choose or write the correct answer.

Strategy   Use your understanding of arrays to solve problems. Sketch an array to show a multiplication problem visually and use the sketch to solve the problem.

10. **Dora says there are two correct ways to solve the number sentence below. The two ways are shown. Is Dora correct? Show why or why not.**

$12 \div 4 \times 3 = ?$

One Way   **Another Way**

$(12 \div 4) \times 3$ $12 \div (4 \times 3)$

Test Tip

Remember, a 6-by-7 array is the same as a 7-by-6 array.

12. **Dimitri has 7 action figures displayed on 6 shelves in his room. Hui has 6 action figures displayed on 7 shelves. Who has more action figures on their shelves? Show your work. Use words, numbers, or pictures.**

11. **Which is NOT a correct way to solve $2 \times 4 \times 3$?**

  (A) First, multiply 2×4, then multiply 2×3, finally add the products.

  (B) First, multiply 2×4, then multiply 8×3.

  (C) First, multiply 2×3, then multiply 6×4.

  (D) First, multiply 4×3, then multiply 12×2.

13. **Which is the same as 9×6? Choose all that apply.**

  (A) $9 \times (4 + 2)$

  (B) $9 \times (3 + 3)$

  (C) $(9 \times 4) + (9 \times 2)$

  (D) $3 \times 3 + (4 \times 2)$

Understand Division as an Unknown Factor Problem

Operations and Algebraic Thinking

Strategy Solve division problems by representing them as unknown factor multiplication problems.

EXAMPLE

Multiplication and division are inverse operations.

$3 \times 9 = 27$ $9 \times 3 = 27$

$27 \div 9 = 3$ $27 \div 3 = 9$

DIRECTIONS: Use the following information to answer questions 1 and 2.

24 students are divided into groups for a playground game. There are 8 students in each group.

1. June knows that $3 \times 8 = 24$. How can she use that fact to find how many groups there are?

_____

_____

_____

_____

2. Write a division equation to solve the problem. Show your work.

_____

_____

3. Tran has 27 apples. He puts 9 apples in each box. Tran wrote the division sentence below to show how many boxes of apples he has. Which number sentence can be used to find the number of boxes?

$$27 \div 9 = \square$$

(A) $9 \times \square = 27$

(B) $27 - 3 = \square$

(C) $9 \times 27 = \square$

(D) $\square \div 9 = 27$

Test Tip

Use what you know about fact families to write related multiplication and division facts.

4. $64 \div 8 = \square$

$8 \times \square = 64$

(A) $\square = 64$

(B) $\square = 56$

(C) $\square = 16$

(D) $\square = 8$

5. Which can be used to find the answer to 30 divided by 5? Choose all that apply.

(A) $35 - 5 = 30$

(B) $6 \times 5 = 30$

(C) $5 + 25 = 30$

(D) $5 \times 6 = 30$

Understand Division as an Unknown Factor Problem

Operations and Algebraic Thinking

Strategy Use division as an unknown factor problem. Find the quotient and one factor to find the unknown factor.

6. Explain how to find the number that makes this number sentence true.

   $36 \div \boxed{} = 9$

   _____

   _____

7. Which operation sign belongs in each box? Write +, −, × or ÷ in the box.

   $42 \boxed{} 7 = 6$ $6 \boxed{} 7 = 42$

   $7 \boxed{} 6 = 42$ $42 \boxed{} 6 = 7$

DIRECTIONS: Use this information to answer questions 8 and 9.

Benita has a bag of 18 fruit slices to share with her 6 friends.

8. Write a division number sentence to find how many slices each friend will get.

   _____

9. Write two multiplication sentences you can use to check your work.

   _____

   _____

10. Leo puts together model cars. He has 13 cars and each car has 3 stickers. Leo wrote the number sentence below to show how many stickers in all are on his 13 cars.

    $13 \times 3 = \boxed{}$

    Write a division number sentence that shows how many stickers are on each car.

    _____

Use Strategies to Multiply and Divide Within 100

Operations and Algebraic Thinking

DIRECTIONS: Choose or write the correct answer.

Strategy | Use your understanding of related operations to find an unknown number or amount. Rewrite multiplication problems as division problems. Rewrite division problems as multiplication problems.

EXAMPLE

Multiplication and division are related operations.

If you know that $6 \times 4 = 24$, then you know that $24 \div 4 = 6$.

1. A dripping faucet leaks 3 gallons of water a day. If the faucet leaks for 9 days, how many gallons of water does the faucet leak?

   (A) 39 gallons

   (B) 27 gallons

   (C) 3 gallons

   (D) 36 gallons

2. Which of the following does NOT equal 9?

   (A) 3×3

   (B) $27 \div 3$

   (C) $2 \times 2 \times 3$

   (D) $18 \div 2$

3. At the grocery store, apples are arranged in 8 rows with 6 apples in each row. How many apples are there in all? Write how you know.

   _____

   _____

   _____

4. If $7 \times 8 = 56$, then $56 \div \boxed{} = 7$

   (A) $\boxed{} = 5$

   (B) $\boxed{} = 6$

   (C) $\boxed{} = 7$

   (D) $\boxed{} = 8$

Test Tip

You can check your answers in a division problem by multiplying your answer by the divisor.

5. Mario solved a problem in math class. He checked his answer by using the number sentence $4 \times 7 = \boxed{}$. Which problem could Mario have been checking?

   (A) $28 \div 7 = \boxed{}$

   (B) $42 \div 7 = \boxed{}$

   (C) $14 \div 7 = \boxed{}$

   (D) $21 \div 7 = \boxed{}$

6. Elli solved $45 \div 9 = \boxed{}$ in math class. Her answer was 5. Write a number sentence Elli could use to check her answer. Was she correct?

Use Strategies to Multiply and Divide Within 100

Operations and Algebraic Thinking

DIRECTIONS: Choose or write the correct answer.

Strategy   Use multiplication and division to solve different kinds of real-life problems. For example, you use multiplication to find area and to convert feet to inches.

7. **What number correctly completes each number sentence?**

   $63 \div 9 = ?$

   $9 \times ? = 63$

   _____

8. **Jonas and Emilio are working on an airplane model. Jonas has a piece of wood that is 15 cm long. His piece is 3 times as long as a piece of wood that Emilio has. How long is Emilio's piece of wood? Show your work.**

10. **How many inches are in 2 feet? (1 foot = 12 inches)**

    (A) 18 inches

    (B) 36 inches

    (C) 24 inches

    (D) 12 inches

11. **Rhea says that $9 \div 1 = 1$. Her answer is wrong. Find the correct answer and write how you know.**

Test Tip

To find the area of a rectangle, multiply the length times the width.

9. **What is the area of this rectangle? Show your work.**

   9 feet

   8 feet

   _____ **square feet**

Solve Two-step Problems: Add, Subtract, Multiply, and Divide

Operations and Algebraic Thinking

DIRECTIONS: Choose or write the correct answer.

> **Strategy** When determining how to solve a problem, break it down into steps. Write the operation needed for each step.

EXAMPLE:

Mike's science class is studying 15 kinds of plants. On Monday, they studied 5 plants and on Tuesday they studied 4 plants. How many plants do they still need to study? Write a number sentence and find the answer.

One way to solve this problem is in two steps.

First, you add. Then, you subtract.

Answer: $15 - (5 + 4) = ?$

$15 - 9 = ?$

$? = 6$

There are 6 plants left to be studied.

1. Isabel, Maria, and Lucas decided to weigh their dogs. The weights are shown in the table below. What is the total weight of the three dogs? Write a number sentence and find the answer.

Isabel's Dog	45 pounds
Maria's Dog	32 pounds
Lucas's Dog	56 pounds

_____

_____

2. Janna invited 15 girls and 13 boys to her party. She plans to give each of her guests 2 balloons and keep one for herself. How many balloons will Janna need in all?

   (A) 28 balloons

   (B) 57 balloons

   (C) 30 balloons

   (D) 29 balloons

3. A music store hopes to have a total of 1,000 customers during the first three months it is open. It had 257 customers the first month and 362 customers the next month. How many customers does the store need during the third month to make its 1,000-customer goal? Show your work.

> **Test Tip**
>
> You can check if your answers are reasonable by estimating.

4. Isabella added 36, 19, and 53. She said that the answer was 137. Is this close to the correct answer? Show how rounding can be used to show why or why not.

5. A dog sitter works for 4 hours and earns $5 an hour. Then, he works 5 hours and earns $6 an hour. Which number sentence shows how to find the amount of money the dog sitter earns all together?

   (A) $4 \times 6 + 5 \times 5 = \square$

   (B) $4 + 5 + 5 + 6 = \square$

   (C) $20 - 5 \times 6 = \square$

   (D) $4 \times 5 + 5 \times 6 = \square$

Solve Two-step Problems: Add, Subtract, Multiply, and Divide
Operations and Algebraic Thinking

DIRECTIONS: Choose or write the correct answer.

Strategy — Look for clue words in a problem that tell you the operation that is needed. For example, *how many* means using addition and *fewer* means subtraction.

6. Chris bakes 3 trays of cookies. Each tray holds 36 cookies. When he takes the cookies out of the oven, he drops 12 cookies. Write and solve a number sentence to find how many cookies Chris has left.

_____

Test Tip

Remember, to find the perimeter of a rectangle, you can add the four sides together or multiply 2 times the length and 2 times the width, and then add.

7. A rectangle has a length of 12 meters and width of 6 meters. Kenji used multiplication and addition to find the perimeter of the rectangle. Show what Kenji's work might look like. Write the answer.

_____

_____

_____

DIRECTIONS: Each package has 5 markers. Use the information that follows to answer questions 8 and 9.

8. Mrs. Chen bought markers. She bought 2 packages of markers for each of the 6 students in her after-school art class. Use the letter *m* to stand for the total number of markers Mrs. Chen bought and write a number sentence that shows this problem.

_____

9. Solve the number sentence to find the total number of markers, *m*, that Mrs. Chen bought.

_____

10. Bianca and her family are taking a car trip. On Friday, they drove 279 miles. On Saturday, they drove 508 miles. Bianca estimated that they drove about a total of 800 miles. Is Bianca correct about the total number of miles driven? Use numbers or words to show why or why not.

_____

_____

_____

_____

_____

_____

11. A store has 476 DVDs on the shelf. The store receives 2 more cases of DVDs, with 100 DVDs in each. How many DVDs does the store have now?

Ⓐ 478 DVDs

Ⓑ 276 DVDs

Ⓒ 676 DVDs

Ⓓ 576 DVDs

Name ______________________________ Date ______________

Math

Identify and Explain Arithmetic Patterns; Addition and Multiplication

Operations and Algebraic Thinking

DIRECTIONS: Choose or write the correct answer.

Strategy Read patterns closely to know if you need to use addition or multiplication. Make sure to use the numbers already provided in the pattern.

Test Tip Arithmetic patterns are patterns that change by the same rate, such as adding the same number.

EXAMPLE

Find the missing number in the table.

IN	3	8	13	19
OUT	5	10		21

First, look for a pattern in the IN and OUT numbers in the table.

Next, decide what operation you need to use to get from the IN number to the OUT number under it.

Then, to get each OUT number, add 2 to the IN number.

So, the missing number in the table is 13 + 2, which is 15.

DIRECTIONS: Use the addition table to answer questions 1–4.

+	1	2	3	4	5	6	7	8	9	10
1	2	3	4	5	6	7	8	9	10	11
2	3	4	5	6	7	8	9	10	11	12
3	4	5	6	7	8	9	10	11	12	13
4	5	6	7	8	9	10	11	12	13	14
5	6	7	8	9	10	11	12	13	14	15
6	7	8	9	10	11	12	13	14	15	16
7	8	9	10	11	12	13	14	15	16	17
8	9	10	11	12	13	14	15	16	17	18
9	10	11	12	13	14	15	16	17	18	19
10	11	12	13	14	15	16	17	18	19	20

1. **What pattern do you see in the sum when you add two EVEN numbers? Write two examples shown in the table.**

____

____

2. **What pattern do you see in the sum when you add two ODD numbers? Write two examples shown in the table.**

____

____

____

3. **Kyle notices that in each column and each row in the addition table, the even and odd numbers take turns, or alternate. Write why this is. Show an example from the table.**

____

____

____

4. **Look at the diagonal line drawn through the 10s in the table. The line shows the different ways of writing 10 as a sum. Write three number sentences with sums of 10 shown in the table.**

____

____

Name _____ Date _____

Identify and Explain Arithmetic Patterns; Addition and Multiplication

Operations and Algebraic Thinking

DIRECTIONS: Use the multiplication table to answer questions 5–8.

Strategy When solving a pattern, try writing number sentences that work for the numbers shown.

×	1	2	3	4	5	6	7	8	9	10
1	1	2	3	4	5	6	7	8	9	10
2	2	4	6	8	10	12	14	16	18	20
3	3	6	9	12	15	18	21	24	27	30
4	4	8	12	16	20	24	28	32	36	40
5	5	10	15	20	25	30	35	40	45	50
6	6	12	18	24	30	36	42	48	54	60
7	7	14	21	28	35	42	49	56	63	70
8	8	16	24	32	40	48	56	64	72	80
9	9	18	27	36	45	54	63	72	81	90
10	10	20	30	40	50	60	70	80	90	100

Test Tip

Apply patterns that use properties of operations, such as the order property of multiplication.

7. **How does the table show that the product of 8 × 7 is the same as the product 7 × 8?**

_____

_____

_____

_____

_____

_____

5. **Describe the pattern you see in the table for multiples of 5 and 10.**

_____

_____

_____

6. **Which is true for all the products of 9 × 1 through 9 × 10?**

(A) When you multiply 9 and an odd number, the product is an even number.

(B) The digit in the tens place is 1 less each time the factor increases by 1.

(C) When you multiply 9 and an even number, the product is an odd number.

(D) The digit in the ones place and the digit in the tens place add up to 9.

8. **Write the missing numbers in the table. Then, tell what the rule is.**

IN	12	16	30	34	44		60
OUT	6	8			22	25	

_____

_____

Math

Round Numbers to the Nearest 10 or 100
Numbers and Operations

DIRECTIONS: Choose or write the correct answer.

Strategy | Apply the rules for rounding to the nearest 10 or 100 when using basic operations that ask for estimates.

Test Tip | Look for key words when solving a problem. If the word *about* is used, an exact answer may not be necessary.

EXAMPLE:

Find the sum of 73 + 48 by rounding the numbers to the nearest 10. Which is correct?

(A) 100 + 40

(B) 100 + 50

(C) 70 + 40

(D) 70 + 50

Answer: D

1. Which of these is the best way to find the answer to this problem by rounding to the nearest 10?

   28 − 19 = ☐

   (A) 30 − 10

   (B) 20 − 10

   (C) 30 − 20

   (D) 10 − 10

2. Round each number to the nearest 10 to find which of the sums is close to 100. Choose all that apply.

   (A) 59 + 57

   (B) 51 + 49

   (C) 39 + 58

   (D) 91 + 8

3. Some people brought their pets to an animal fair. 133 people brought dogs. 180 people brought cats. 110 people brought other pets. About how many people brought pets to the fair? Solve the problem by rounding the numbers to the nearest 100. Show your work.

4. What is 34,571 rounded to the nearest 100?

   (A) 34,000

   (B) 35,500

   (C) 34,600

   (D) 34,570

5. Lisa, Jana, and Corey weighed pumpkins they had grown during the summer. The weights are shown in the table below. To the nearest 100, about how much do the pumpkins weigh all together? Show how you know.

Lisa's Pumpkin	184 pounds
Jana's Pumpkin	289 pounds
Corey's Pumpkin	304 pounds

Round Numbers to the Nearest 10 or 100
Numbers and Operations

DIRECTIONS: Choose or write the correct answer.

Strategy   Use the rules for rounding up or down as you solve problems requiring estimation.

Test Tip   When rounding to the nearest 100, if the value of the number in the tens place is less than 5, round the number down.

6. Josela collected 578 plastic water bottles to recycle.

578 rounded to the nearest 10 is _____ .

7. Look at the numbers in the box below. Which number, when rounded to the nearest 100, rounds to 600? Write how you know.

        498, 579, 668, 536

_____

_____

_____

_____

_____

_____

8. Round to the tens and hundreds place. Write each number in the correct box.

Number	Rounded to the Nearest 10	Rounded to the Nearest 100
315		
1,068		
72		
	340	300

9. Mr. Ames is the grocery store manager. He counts all the customers that come into the store one day and rounds the number to the closest hundred. He rounds to 800. Which of these could be the original number of customers? Choose all that apply.

(A) 831

(B) 897

(C) 767

(D) 749

Add and Subtract Within 1,000
Numbers and Operations

DIRECTIONS: Choose or write the correct answer.

Strategy When adding and subtracting larger numbers, line them up by place value to make sure your answer is correct.

EXAMPLE

There are 134 students on the playground and 254 students inside the school. What is the total number of students?

One way to add:

$100 + 200 = 300$

$30 + 50 = 80$

$4 + 4 = 8$

$300 + 80 + 8 = 388$ students

1. What is the missing number in this number sentence?

   $248 + 672 = \Box$

   (A) 224
   (B) 324
   (C) 920
   (D) 334

2. A truck driver makes deliveries between two cities. The cities are 534 miles apart. He has already driven 165 miles. How many more miles does he have to go?

   (A) 431 miles
   (B) 469 miles
   (C) 489 miles
   (D) 369 miles

3. Jeffrey explained how to add 168 and 115. He made a mistake. What mistake did Jeffrey make?

   Jeffrey's Way

   • Add 2 to 168 to get 170.
   • Add 110 to 170 to get 280.
   • The sum is 280.

4. The number of people watching a high school football game is 732. At half time, 56 people leave. How many people are left watching the game?

   (A) 724 people
   (B) 684 people
   (C) 676 people
   (D) 686 people

5. Callie, Alyssa, and Nina count stickers in their collections. The numbers are shown in the table below. How many stickers do the girls have all together? Show how you know.

Callie's Stickers	38
Alyssa's Stickers	115
Nina's Stickers	89

Test Tip

Check your answer to see if it makes sense.

Add and Subtract Within 1,000
Numbers and Operations

Strategy Use your understanding of place value and regrouping to add and subtract correctly.

6. **Which number sentence can be used to check the sum of this problem?**

   278
   + 53

   (A) 331 − 53 = 278
   (B) 278 − 53 = 225
   (C) 321 − 53 = 268
   (D) 231 − 53 = 178

Test Tip

If any place has more than 9, then regrouping is needed.

9. **Which number, when added to 456, makes a problem that needs regrouping in ones, tens, and hundreds?**

   _____

10. **Write the sums for the problems in questions 7, 8, and 9.**

    _____

DIRECTIONS: Use the numbers below to answer questions 7–9.

   544, 222, 325, 344

7. **Which number, when added to 456, makes a problem that needs no regrouping?**

   _____

8. **Which number, when added to 456, makes a problem that needs regrouping in the ones and tens only?**

   _____

Multiply One-Digit Whole Numbers by Multiples of 10
Numbers and Operations

DIRECTIONS: Choose or write the correct answer.

Strategy | Use basic multiplication facts and your understanding of place value to find products involving multiples of ten.

EXAMPLE

What is the product: 20 × 7 = ☐

First, multiply 2 × 7.

2 × 7 = 14

Then, multiply 14 by 10.

14 × 10 = 140

So, 20 × 7 = 140

Test Tip

Look at each answer choice carefully before choosing an answer.

1. **What is 4 × 90?**
   - Ⓐ 36
   - Ⓑ 3,600
   - Ⓒ 360
   - Ⓓ 94

2. **Carlos multiplies 4 × 70. How many groups of 100 should be in his answer? Write how you know.**

   _____

   _____

   _____

3. **There are 40 cars on the car lot. Each car has 4 wheels. How many wheels are there in all?**
   - Ⓐ 120
   - Ⓑ 160
   - Ⓒ 44
   - Ⓓ 200

4. **The picture below shows a group of 10 chairs around a table. How many chairs are in 5 of these groups?**

   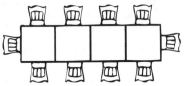

5. **A music store ordered 400 new CDs. The store did not know how many boxes or how many CDs there would be in each box of the order. Which number sentence shows the possible number of boxes and CDs per box to equal 400? Choose all that apply.**
   - Ⓐ 4 × 100 = ☐
   - Ⓑ 5 × 80 = ☐
   - Ⓒ 10 × 4 = ☐
   - Ⓓ 10 × 40 = ☐

Multiply One-Digit Whole Numbers by Multiples of 10
Numbers and Operations

Strategy   As you read a word problem, write an equation with basic operations to help you understand how to answer the question.

6. Maddie multiplies 6 × 80. How many groups of 100 are in her answer?

_____

_____

_____

7. Kimiko multiplies 60 by 5 and gets the product 3,000. Is Kimiko's answer correct? Show why or why not.

_____

_____

_____

_____

Test Tip

Remember, there are 60 seconds in one minute, 60 minutes in an hour, and 24 hours in a day.

8. Zoey can read 8 pages of her younger brother's book in 4 minutes. How many seconds is this? Show your work.

9. Marta spends 6 hours working on a class project. How many minutes is this? Show your work.

_____

_____

10. 360 students want to go on the school trip. There are 7 buses for the trip and each bus holds 50 students. Is there enough room on the buses for all the students to go on the class trip? Write how you know.

_____

_____

_____

Understand Unit Fractions
Numbers and Operations

DIRECTIONS: Choose or write the correct answer.

Strategy
Use visuals to help you work with fractions. If needed, draw a circle divided into the number shown in the bottom of the fraction, and shade in the parts of the number shown on the top of the fraction.

Test Tip
To find the fraction of a whole, count the number of equal parts. The bottom number of the fraction is the number of equal parts. The top number is how many of these parts.

EXAMPLE

Which fraction shows how much of this figure is shaded?

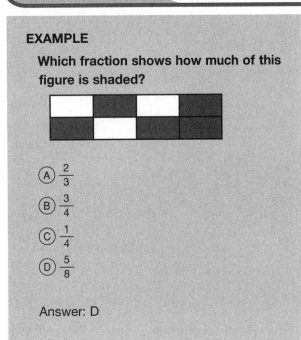

Ⓐ $\frac{2}{3}$

Ⓑ $\frac{3}{4}$

Ⓒ $\frac{1}{4}$

Ⓓ $\frac{5}{8}$

Answer: D

1. Which picture represents the fraction $\frac{3}{4}$?

Ⓐ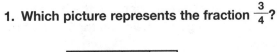

Ⓑ

Ⓒ

Ⓓ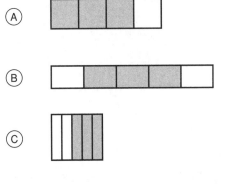

2. Miguel says that $\frac{2}{3}$ of this rectangle is shaded. Is Miguel correct? Explain why or why not.

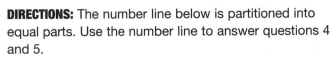

_____

_____

_____

3. What fraction is shown by the shaded part of the square? Write how you know.

_____

_____

DIRECTIONS: The number line below is partitioned into equal parts. Use the number line to answer questions 4 and 5.

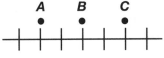

4. Which point shows $\frac{2}{8}$?

_____

5. Which point shows $\frac{6}{8}$?

_____

Understand Unit Fractions

Numbers and Operations

Strategy Use pictures as tools that you can use to solve fractions. Study a picture carefully to be sure you understand what it represents.

6. **Which fraction is shown by the unshaded part of the circle?**

(A) $\frac{4}{6}$

(B) $\frac{2}{6}$

(C) $\frac{1}{6}$

(D) $\frac{6}{6}$

7. **Which rectangle is divided into fourths? Choose all that apply.**

 (A)

(B)

(C)

(D)

DIRECTIONS: Use the pictures of the pizzas below to answer questions 8 and 9.

_____

_____

_____

8. **Sara, Ben, and Lara each ate part of a pizza. Sara ate $\frac{1}{2}$ of a pizza. Ben ate $\frac{4}{8}$ of a pizza. Lara ate $\frac{1}{3}$ of a pizza. Write the name of each person under the pizza that they ate.**

9. **Who ate more pizza? Write how you know.**

_____

_____

_____

Represent Fractions on a Number Line
Numbers and Operations

DIRECTIONS: Choose or write the correct answer.

Strategy Use graphs, tables, and drawings to understand data.

1. Tomas and Fabio were sharing one pizza. Tomas ate $\frac{3}{8}$ of the pizza and Fabio ate $\frac{5}{8}$. Tomas drew the number line below to show how much he and Fabio ate. Is the number line correct? Write how you know.

_____

_____

_____

Test Tip

Read a number line from left to right. The values get greater the farther right you go.

2. On a number line, is $\frac{2}{3}$ to the right or left of $\frac{1}{3}$? Write how you know.

_____

_____

_____

_____

DIRECTIONS: The number line below is partitioned into equal parts. Use the number line to answer questions 3 and 4.

3. Complete the number line. Write the correct fractions on the lines.

4. Draw a point on the number line to show $\frac{4}{6}$.

DIRECTIONS: Use the number line below to answer questions 5 and 6.

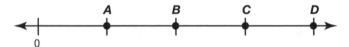

5. Which point shows $\frac{4}{4}$?
   - (A) Point A
   - (B) Point B
   - (C) Point C
   - (D) Point D

6. What fraction is located at Point *B*?

_____

Represent Fractions on a Number Line
Numbers and Operations

DIRECTIONS: Use the number line below to answer questions 7–9.

Strategy   Use number lines as tools to help you read fractions.

Test Tip   To read fractions on a number line, count the equal intervals between 0 and 1.

7. Van cut his fruit bar into thirds. He ate 2 of the 3 parts of the bar. Draw a point on the number line to show the part of the fruit bar Van ate.

8. Write the fraction above the point.

9. Write why you placed the point where you did.

_____

_____

_____

_____

_____

_____

10. Neal and Lars are sharing the duty of cutting their family's lawn. Neal cuts $\frac{2}{6}$ of the lawn and Lars cuts $\frac{4}{6}$ of the lawn. Which number line correctly shows the fractional amount each boy cuts?

Ⓐ
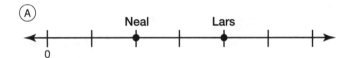

Ⓑ

Ⓒ
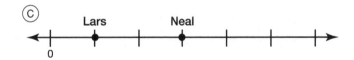

Ⓓ
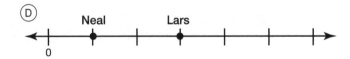

Use Fraction Models and Number Lines to Generate Equivalent Fractions
Numbers and Operations

DIRECTIONS: Choose or write the correct answer.

Strategy Look at the shaded parts of graphs, tables, and drawings to understand parts of a whole.

1. The shape below has $\frac{1}{3}$ shaded. Which shape has a shaded amount equal to $\frac{1}{3}$?

Ⓐ

Ⓑ

Ⓒ

Ⓓ

DIRECTIONS: Use the information below to answer questions 2–5.

Isabel plants a flower garden and a vegetable garden of equal size. She plants $\frac{2}{4}$ of her flower garden with daisies and $\frac{4}{8}$ of her vegetable garden with peppers.

2. Shade the rectangle to show how much of Isabel's flower garden is planted with daisies.

3. Shade the rectangle to show how much of Isabel's vegetable garden is planted with peppers.

4. Write a number sentence using <, =, or > to compare the fraction of the flower garden that is planted with daisies and the fraction of the vegetable garden that is planted with peppers.

_____

_____

5. Write how you know your number sentence is correct.

_____

_____

_____

Name _____ Date _____

Math

Compare Fractions by Size
Numbers and Operations

DIRECTIONS: Use the picture below to answer questions 6 and 7.

Strategy   Compare fractional amounts by drawing or visualizing them as parts of a whole object.

Test Tip   To compare amounts, be sure the wholes are the same size.

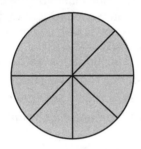

6. Write the two fractions shown by the shaded parts.

_____

_____

7. Write a number sentence to compare the fractions. Use <, =, or >.

_____

_____

_____

8. Eva and Carmen each ate $\frac{1}{3}$ of their pizza. Who ate more? Write how you know.

Eva's Pizza

Carmen's Pizza

_____

_____

_____

_____

Math

Tell and Write Time to the Nearest Minute
Measurement and Data

DIRECTIONS: Choose or write the correct answer.

Strategy — Read different types of clocks in order to tell time and answer questions about time.

EXAMPLE

Jessica baked bread. This clock shows the time she put the bread in the oven.

This clock shows the time Jessica took the bread out of the oven.

How many minutes did Jessica bake her bread?

Answer: 42 minutes

1. Xavier left home at 7:30 a.m. to go to school. It took him 8 minutes to walk to the bus stop. There, he waited for 5 minutes for the bus to arrive. The bus ride to school took 17 minutes. What time did Xavier get to school?

   Ⓐ 7:43 a.m.
   Ⓑ 7:47 a.m.
   Ⓒ 7:55 a.m.
   Ⓓ 8:00 a.m.

2. What time does the clock show? Choose all that apply.

   Ⓐ 5 minutes past 5:00
   Ⓑ 18 minutes past 5:00
   Ⓒ 42 minutes before 6:00
   Ⓓ 18 minutes before 5:00

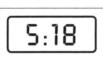

Test Tip

The large marks on the clock indicate 5 minutes. The small marks on the clock indicate 1 minute each. Count by 5s and 1s to find how much time has elapsed.

3. Martin looked at the clock before he started his running practice. Then, he checked it again when he finished. How much time passed between Martin's start time and finish time? Explain how you know.

   Start Time   End Time

   _____

   _____

   _____

4. Look at the clock. How much time will it take for the minute hand to reach one minute past the 12?

   Ⓐ 1 minute
   Ⓑ 15 minutes
   Ⓒ 45 minutes
   Ⓓ 46 minutes

5. Luisa finished her homework at 8:16 p.m. It took Luisa 36 minutes to do her homework. What time did Luisa start her homework? Show how you know.

Name _____   Date _____

Math

Tell and Write Time to the Nearest Minute
Measurement and Data

DIRECTIONS: Use the information below to answer questions 6 and 7.

Strategy   You can use a number line to represent time problems that involve adding and subtracting minutes.

Sometimes, Shiro's clock does not show the correct time. Shiro left the park at 6:15 p.m. and walked 15 minutes to the store. Five minutes later, he got on a bus and rode 23 minutes. Shiro then walked 5 minutes to his house. Shiro's clock below shows the time that he arrived home.

6. Does Shiro's clock show the correct time

_____

7. Show how you know.

_____

_____

_____

_____

_____

_____

8. Akiko arrived at Liam's party at 2:45 p.m. She left her house 19 minutes before she arrived at the party. She stopped to buy some party supplies 7 minutes after she left her house, as shown on the number line below. What time did Akiko stop to buy the party supplies?

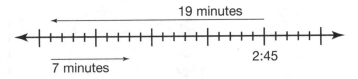

DIRECTIONS: Use the clock below to answer questions 9 and 10.

9. Write numbers in the blank clock to show the time 15 minutes BEFORE the time shown.

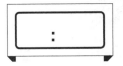

10. Write numbers in the blank clock to show the time 15 minutes AFTER the time shown.

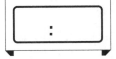

Liquid Volume and Mass: Grams, Kilograms, Liters
Measurement and Data

DIRECTIONS: Choose or write the correct answer.

Strategy Choose the right tool and units to measure and estimate liquid volume and mass.

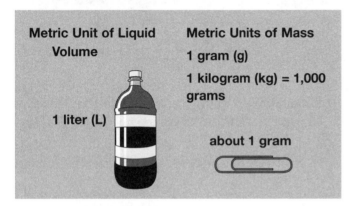

Metric Unit of Liquid Volume

1 liter (L)

Metric Units of Mass

1 gram (g)

1 kilogram (kg) = 1,000 grams

about 1 gram

1. A hot dog weighs about _____.

- (A) 2 grams
- (B) 2 pounds
- (C) 16 ounces
- (D) 56 grams

2. Look at the picture of the quarter. Is the best estimate of the mass of the quarter 5 kilograms or 5 grams? Tell how you found the answer.

_____

_____

_____

_____

_____

3. Which object is most likely to have a mass of about 2 kilograms?

(A)

(B)

(C)

(D)

Test Tip

Remember, a bottle of the size below holds about 1 liter of liquid.

4. The pot below holds 6 liters of water. Lia needs to fill the pot with water to make soup. She fills the bottle below 3 times and says she has filled the pot. Is Lia correct? Tell why or why not. Show how you know.

_____

Math

Solve One-Step Problems: Mass and Volume
Measurement and Data

DIRECTIONS: Choose or write the correct answer.

> **Strategy** Use basic operations to solve problems involving measurements. Read the problems carefully to decide which operation to use. Draw pictures if needed.

1. **Lila has 4 new pencils that together weigh 20 grams. How much does one pencil weigh?**

   Ⓐ 4 grams

   Ⓑ 5 grams

   Ⓒ 15 grams

   Ⓓ 20 grams

2. **Bennett buys 4 watermelons with the same mass as the one shown below. What is the mass of the 4 watermelons Bennett buys? Show how you know.**

   mass = 4 kg

   _____

   _____

   _____

3. **Which of the following problems have an answer of 12 liters? Choose all that apply.**

   Ⓐ Cans of juice are sold in 6-packs. If each 6-pack of juice has a total of 3 liters of juice, how many liters of juice are in 4 6-packs of juice?

   Ⓑ A bottle of water holds 2 liters. How many liters of water are there in 5 bottles?

   Ⓒ Sophia fills 6 water bottles with water for her friends for a camping trip. If each bottle holds 2 liters of water, how many liters of water has Sophia used to fill the bottles?

   Ⓓ Darius has a bucket that holds 1 liter of water. He fills and empties it 12 times to fill his fish tank. How much water did Darius use to fill the tank?

DIRECTIONS: Use the three containers below to answer questions 4 and 5.

> **Test Tip**
> Remember, the larger the container, the more it will hold.

A   B   C

4. **Will it take more of Item A or Item C to fill the pot? Tell how you know.**

   _____

   _____

   _____

   _____

5. **If the bottle holds 2 liters of water and the pot, when filled, holds 9 liters, how many bottles of water will be needed to fill the post? How much water is left over?**

   _____

   _____

   _____

   _____

Math

Draw Picture Graphs and Bar Graphs
Measurement and Data

DIRECTIONS: Choose or write the correct answer.

Strategy   When viewing graphs, tables, and drawings, read the labels and captions carefully to make sure you understand the data shown.

Test Tip   A scaled pictograph includes symbols that represent multiple units. In a scaled bar graph, each interval also represents multiple units, such as 5.

1. **The data in the table below shows a person's heart rate while jogging. Use the data to complete the bar graph. Draw bars to show the data.**

Time	Heart Rate
0 min.	80
5 min.	120
10 min.	130
15 min.	150
20 min.	160
25 min.	150

Test Tip   Remember, if your scale counts by 2s, you can use half a picture to show numbers in between.

2. **Use the data in the table below to complete the picture graph about favorite snacks. Draw pictures to show the data. Complete the key to show what each picture stands for.**

Snack Type	Number
Cookie	6
Carrot sticks	1
Chips	3
Banana	4
Apple	2

Bar Graph
Heart Rate While Jogging

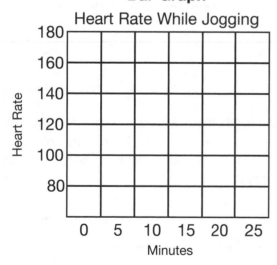

Snack Type	Number
Cookie	
Carrot sticks	
Chips	
Banana	
Apple	

Key: _____ = 2 students

Solve Problems Using Bar Graphs
Measurement and Data

Strategy | If you don't understand the data in a graph, table, or drawing, take the information and try drawing a different visual. Or, make a table with the information.

DIRECTIONS: Use the bar graph below to answer questions 1–3.

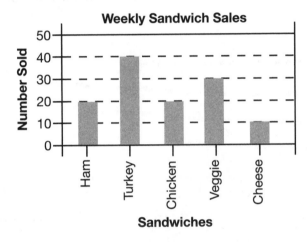

1. How many more turkey sandwiches were sold than chicken sandwiches during the week?

_____

2. What kinds of sandwiches were sold more than cheese sandwiches but less than veggie sandwiches?

_____

3. How many sandwiches in all were sold?

_____

DIRECTIONS: Use the Heart Rate While Jogging bar graph you made on page 90 to answer questions 4–6.

4. At what time was the jogger's heart rate the highest? Show how you know.

_____

_____

_____

5. At which times was the jogger's heart rate the same?

_____

Test Tip

An interval is the amount of time between two events. On the Heart Rate While Jogging graph, it is the time between each heart rate.

6. During which time interval did the jogger's heart rate increase the most?

Ⓐ 0 minutes to 5 minutes

Ⓑ 10 minutes to 15 minutes

Ⓒ 15 minutes to 20 minutes

Ⓓ 20 minutes to 25 minutes

Measure Length and Show Data on a Line Plot
Measurement and Data

DIRECTIONS: Choose or write the correct answer.

> **Strategy** Look for what graphs, tables, and drawings are comparing. Most graphs and tables compare more than one object.

1. Zuri has some lengths of ribbon that she will weave together. The ribbons are shown below. Measure the lengths in inches and write the measures.

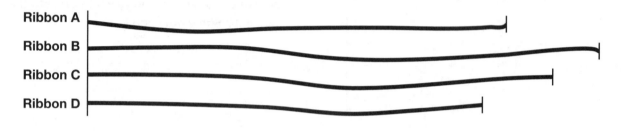

_____

_____

2. Zuri has already measured some lengths of ribbon as shown in the table below.

Length (inches)	Number of Ribbons
3	4
3 1/4	2
3 1/2	4
4	5
5	7
5 1/2	6

> **Test Tip**
> The first and last measures on a line plot should be the greatest and least values in the data.

Make a line plot of all the ribbon lengths. Use the lengths you measured and the measures in the table to complete the line plot below. Write on the lines the first value and the last value of the data. Draw Xs to show the data.

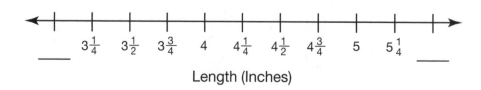

Length (Inches)

Name _____ Date _____

Math

Finding Area: Unit Squares
Measurement and Data

DIRECTIONS: Choose or write the correct answer.

Strategy

Use unit squares to find area.

EXAMPLE

The area of a figure can be found by finding the total number of same-size units of area required to cover the shape without gaps or overlaps. The area of the figure below is 4 square units.

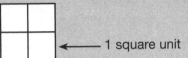 ← 1 square unit

Test Tip

Count the square units to find the area.

1. What is the area of this figure?

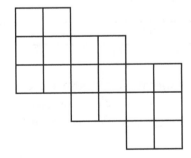

A) 14 square units

B) 16 square units

C) 22 square units

D) 18 square units

DIRECTIONS: Look at the figure below. The side of each square represents 1 inch. Use the figure to answer questions 2–4.

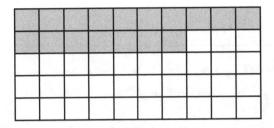

2. What is the area of the shaded part of the figure?

_____

3. What is the area of the unshaded part of the figure?

_____

4. What is the area of the whole figure? Show how you know.

_____

_____

5. LuAnn says that the shaded part of the figure below has a greater area than the unshaded part. Is LuAnn correct? Write how you know.

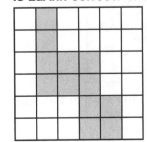 = 1 square centimeter

_____

_____

_____

Relate Finding Area to Multiplication and Addition
Measurement and Data

DIRECTIONS: Choose or write the correct answer.

EXAMPLE

To find the area of the figure, you can count the total number of squares or multiply 4 x 5.

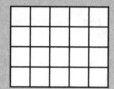

There are 20 squares: 4 × 5 = 20

The area of the figure is 20 square units.

DIRECTIONS: Use the figure below to answer questions 1 and 2.

Test Tip

Multiplying the side lengths of a rectangle gives the same measurement of area as counting the number of square units inside the rectangle.

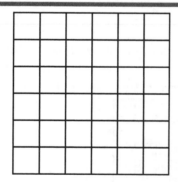

1. **Which can be used to find the area of this figure? Choose all that apply.**

   (A) = 6 × 6

   (B) = 5 × 4

   (C) = 6 + 6

   (D) = 6 + 6 + 6 + 6 + 6 + 6

2. **What is the area of the figure? Write how you know.**

   _____

3. **Sherrine and her mom have a tablecloth that has an area of 20 square feet. They want to cover the table top shown below with the tablecloth. Is the tablecloth large enough to cover the table top? Show how you know.**

   3 feet

   6 feet

   _____

   _____

DIRECTIONS: Use the figure below to answer questions 4 and 5.

   1 cm

   9 cm

4. **Donnell fills the rectangle with 1-centimeter-square tiles. How many centimeter-square tiles will fill the rectangle, with no overlaps?**

   (A) 10

   (B) 9

   (C) 19

   (D) 20

5. **What is the area of the figure? Show 2 ways to find the area.**

   _____

   _____

Relate Finding Area to Multiplication and Addition
Measurement and Data

DIRECTIONS: Choose or write the correct answer.

Strategy   Use multiplication and addition to find the areas of figures in square units.

DIRECTIONS: Mr. Miller drew the figure below on the board. Use the figure to answer questions 6 and 7.

6. **Levon says the area of the figure is 18 square units. He counted the squares around the outside of the figure. Mr. Miller tells Levon he did not find the area of the figure correctly. What did Levon do wrong? Include the correct area in your answer.**

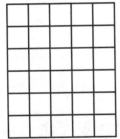

_____

_____

_____

_____

_____

7. **Show how you can use multiplication to find the area of Mr. Miller's figure.**

_____

_____

_____

Test Tip

You can find the area of some figures by separating them into non-overlapping rectangles and adding together the areas of the non-overlapping rectangles.

8. **Alyssa wrote a number sentence to find the area of her figure. The number sentence uses multiplication and addition. Write the number sentence Alyssa could have written.**

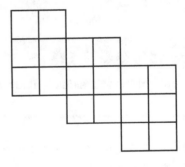

_____

_____

Solve Problems: Perimeter
Measurement and Data

DIRECTIONS: Choose or write the correct answer.

Strategy Use addition to find the perimeters of figures. Identify the number of sides a figure has and the length of each side. Then, add to find the perimeter.

EXAMPLE

Perimeter is the distance around the edge of a shape.

You can add to find the perimeter.

Width = 5 ft

Length = 18 ft

5 + 5 + 18 + 18 = 46

The perimeter is 46 feet.

Test Tip

Add the lengths of the four sides to find the perimeter.

1. A rectangle has a length of 27 feet and a width of 2 feet. What is the perimeter?

   (A) 27 feet

   (B) 58 feet

   (C) 29 feet

   (D) 54 feet

2. A rectangle has a perimeter of 24 feet. Which can be the side measures of the rectangle? Choose all that apply.

   (A) length: 10 feet; width 2 feet

   (B) length: 11 feet; width 1 foot

   (C) length: 12 feet; width 3 feet

   (D) length: 7 feet; width 5 feet

3. The triangle below has a perimeter of 37 inches. What is the length of the bottom of the triangle? Show how you found your answer.

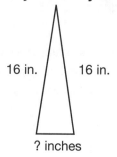

16 in.   16 in.

? inches

_____

_____

_____

Test Tip

To find the perimeter of a rectangle, you can double the lengths of the sides next to each other and then, add them together.

4. Jack drew two rectangles, A and B, shown below. They have the same perimeter. Jack says they also have the same area. Is Jack correct? Show how you know.

4 meters

5 meters

3 meters

6 meters

_____

Math

Describe Properties of Shapes and Identify Quadrilaterals

Geometry

DIRECTIONS: Choose or write the correct answer.

> **Strategy**   Use the characteristics of different shapes to identify them.

EXAMPLE

A quadrilateral is a figure with 4 straight sides and 4 angles.

A trapezoid is a quadrilateral.

Test Tip

Read each question carefully. Look for key words and numbers that will help you find the correct answer.

1. Which of these shapes is NOT a quadrilateral?

(A)

(B)

(C)

(D)

3. How many sides does a quadrilateral have?

(A) 3 sides

(B) 4 sides

(C) 5 sides

(D) 6 sides

4. A 4-sided shape that has only one pair of parallel sides is called a _____. Choose all that apply.

(A) parallelogram

(B) quadrilateral

(C) hexagon

(D) trapezoid

Test Tip

To determine the name of a shape, look at its properties.

2. Look at the shapes. How are they alike? How are they different?

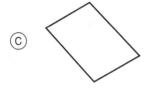

_____

_____

5. What shape has fewer sides than a square?

_____

Describe Properties of Shapes
and Identify Quadrilaterals
Geometry

DIRECTIONS: Choose or write the correct answer.

Strategy   To understand a word problem about shapes, draw what is described.

6. Which BEST describes the shape of the dollar bill?

(A) circle

(B) rhombus

(C) rectangle

(D) square

7. Jamal wrote the riddle below. What is the answer to his riddle? Show how you know.

I have 4 sides and 4 corners.

My sides are parallel.

My corners are not right angles.

What shape am I?

_____

_____

_____

8. Look at the group of quadrilaterals below.

Mr. Graham asked Su Pak to draw a quadrilateral that cannot be grouped with these shapes. She drew the shape shown below.

Write how you know the quadrilateral Su Pak drew does not belong in the same group as the other quadrilaterals.

9. Which is an example of a parallelogram? Choose all that apply.

(A) rhombus

(B) cone

(C) trapezoid

(D) rectangle

Partition Shapes into Parts
Geometry

DIRECTIONS: Choose or write the correct answer.

 Strategy Make a chart or list with the numbers, shapes, and measurements to help you understand how to answer the question.

This shape is partitioned into 4 equal parts. Each part is $\frac{1}{4}$ of the whole.

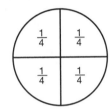

1. Paulo shaded $\frac{1}{4}$ of a shape. Which shape could be Paulo's? Choose all that apply.

Ⓐ

Ⓑ

Ⓒ

Ⓓ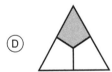

2. How many equal parts are in the rectangle?

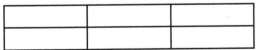

DIRECTIONS: Andrew drew these two same-sized rectangles and divided each into equal parts. Use the shapes to answer questions 3 and 4.

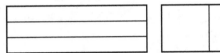

3. Andrew says that each of the parts have the same area. Is Andrew correct? Write how you know.

_____

4. What is the fractional name of each part?

_____

Test Tip

Read each question carefully. Look for key words and numbers that will help you find the correct answer.

5. What fraction shows the shaded part of the circle?

Ⓐ $\frac{1}{4}$

Ⓑ $\frac{4}{3}$

Ⓒ $\frac{3}{4}$

Ⓓ $\frac{1}{3}$

6. Mr. Halley told Lana to shade $\frac{3}{6}$ of the rectangle. Did Lana shade the rectangle correctly? Write how you know.

Strategy Review

In this section, you will review the strategies you learned and apply them to practice the skills.

Strategy Use basic operations to solve problems.

EXAMPLE:

At Washington Elementary School, folding chairs are stored in a large closet. Mary Jo needs to set up 9 rows of folding chairs for a talent show. She plans to put 8 chairs in each row. How many chairs should she get out of the closet?

First, write a number sentence.

$9 \times 8 = \square$

Then, solve your number sentence.

$9 \times 8 = 72$

Mary Jo needs to get 72 chairs out of the closet.

1. Selene works at her family's stand at the farmer's market. She has 56 peaches. She needs to place 7 peaches in each container. What number sentence can Selene use to find how many peaches to place in each bag?

   (A) $7 \times 56 = \square$

   (B) $56 - 7 = \square$

   (C) $7 + 56 = \square$

   (D) $56 \div 7 = \square$

   How many containers of peaches can she fill?

   _____

2. The table shows the cost of tickets for an art museum. The Marsel family includes two adults and three children. Use the information in the table to find how much it cost the family to visit the museum. Show your work.

Type of Ticket	Cost ($)
Adult	15
Child	8

3. The drama club meets three times a month. How many times do they meet each year?

   (A) 30 times

   (B) 33 times

   (C) 36 times

   (D) 39 times

4. A group of students is going on a field trip. There are 5 buses. 52 students can fit on each bus. Which number sentence can be used to find out how many students can go on the field trip?

   (A) $5 \times 52 = \square$

   (B) $52 - 5 = \square$

   (C) $5 + 52 = \square$

   (D) $52 \div 5 = \square$

5. Lee is making gift bags for a party. She will place 4 small gifts in each bag. She has a total of 48 gifts. Write a number sentence you can use to find the total number of gift bags Lee can make. Show your work.

Name _____ Date _____

Math

Strategy Review

Strategy — Use what you know about numbers, shapes, and measurement to answer questions.

EXAMPLE:

Janice measures one side of a square. She finds that the side is 6 inches. How can she find the area of the square?

First, recall that a square has four equal sides.

Then, find the area of the square by multiplying the length by the width: 6 in. × 6 in. = 36 square inches.

EXAMPLE:

River finds the perimeter of a triangle with sides 3 in., 4 in., and 5 in. He says the perimeter is 12 square inches. Is he correct?

First, add the side length to find the sum: 3 + 4 + 5 = 12.

Then, include the correct units in the answer: centimeters.

The perimeter is 12 centimeters.

River is incorrect, because perimeter is not measured in square units.

1. What is the area and perimeter of the shape shown below? Show your work.

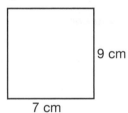

9 cm

7 cm

Area:

Perimeter:

2. The perimeter of the triangle below is 24 feet. What is the missing measurement?

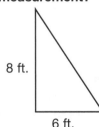

8 ft.

6 ft.

(A) 8 ft.
(B) 9 ft.
(C) 10 ft.
(D) 18 ft.

3. A shape has two pairs of parallel sides. Which could be the shape? Choose all that apply.

(A) square
(B) trapezoid
(C) rectangle
(D) parallelogram

4. Sara found the area of a rectangle. Which of these could be the area of the rectangle? Choose all that apply.

(A) 6 square feet
(B) 6 centimeters
(C) 6 square inches
(D) 6 pounds

5. Eben found the mass of an apple. Which of these could be the mass of the apple?

(A) 200 liters
(B) 200 grams
(C) 200 pounds
(D) 200 inches

Strategy Review

Strategy Read word problems carefully. Make sure you know what you are asked to do.

EXAMPLE:

A florist is making flower arrangements for a graduation party. He has 10 vases. In each vase, he places five yellow carnations and 4 purple carnations. He fills in the empty space with small white flowers. How many purple flowers does he use for the party?

First, think about what you know from the word problem. You know the number of vases and the number of yellow and purple flowers in each vase.

Next, think about what you are being asked to find. You need to find the number of purple flowers used in 10 vases. Notice that you do not need to find the number of yellow flowers, or the total number of flowers.

Then, write and solve a number sentence: $10 \times 4 = 40$.

He uses 40 purple flowers.

1. A baker is making cupcakes for a birthday. She makes 24 cupcakes. Half are frosted green and half are frosted white. The baker places four blue candies on top of each white cupcake. How many blue candies will the baker use?

   Ⓐ 24
   Ⓑ 36
   Ⓒ 48
   Ⓓ 96

If the baker buys the candies in packs of 10, and has 5 packs, will she have enough to complete the cupcakes? Explain how you found the answer.

_____

_____

_____

2. Jake is cutting a loaf of bread into equal slices. The loaf is 10 inches long. He wants to make sure there are at least 12 slices. Will each slice be less than or greater than one inch in width?

_____

How do you know?

_____

_____

3. Ella has three dogs, and feeds each one two cups of dog food per day. How many cups of dog food will she feed all three dogs in a week?

   Ⓐ 5 cups
   Ⓑ 6 cups
   Ⓒ 36 cups
   Ⓓ 42 cups

4. Noelle lives 2 miles from her school. She bikes to school and home each school day. She also bikes from her home to the library and back twice a week. The library is 1 mile from Noelle's home. How many miles does Noelle bike on a normal week? Show your work.

Name _____ Date _____

Math

Strategy Review

| **Strategy** | Use graphs, tables, and drawings to understand numbers. |

EXAMPLE

Shana has 1 pound of butter. She uses $\frac{1}{2}$ pound to make biscuits. She used another $\frac{1}{4}$ pound for a pie crust. How much butter did she use? Shade the rectangle to show how much she used. Then, use your shaded rectangle to find how much was left.

First, shade in the faction of the butter that she used for the biscuits:

Then, shade in the fraction she used for the pie:

She used $\frac{3}{4}$ pound of butter.

$\frac{1}{4}$ pound was left.

1. Lorne drew the number line below to solve a problem.

0   1

Which of the following could be the problem Lorne solved?

Ⓐ A teacher made 2 gallons of lemonade. He used $\frac{1}{2}$ gallon to fill cups for the students. How much lemonade was left?

Ⓑ A teacher made 1 gallon of lemonade. He used $\frac{2}{3}$ gallon to fill cups for the students. How much lemonade was left?

Ⓒ A teacher made 2 gallons of lemonade. He used $\frac{2}{3}$ gallon to fill cups for the students. How much lemonade was left?

Ⓓ A teacher made 1 gallon of lemonade. He used $\frac{1}{2}$ gallon to fill cups for the students. How much lemonade was left?

2. Jay, Maddy, and Evan share two pizzas. Each pizza is cut into 6 equal pieces. Maddy eats three pieces, Jay eats two pieces, and Evan eats three pieces. How many pieces of pizza are left? Draw a picture to help you find an answer.

3. Eric and Toby each ordered a sandwich. Eric ate $\frac{2}{3}$ of his sandwich. Toby ate $\frac{3}{4}$ of his sandwich. Who ate a greater amount of his sandwich? Draw a picture and show your work.

4. Mr. and Mrs. Barrett are painting their basement walls. On Tuesday, they painted $\frac{1}{3}$ of the walls. On Wednesday, they painted $\frac{1}{3}$ more of the walls. If they want to finish the job on Thursday, what fraction of the walls will they need to paint? Draw a picture and show your work.

Ask and Answer Questions
Reading: Literature

DIRECTIONS: Read the story. Then, choose or write the best answer.

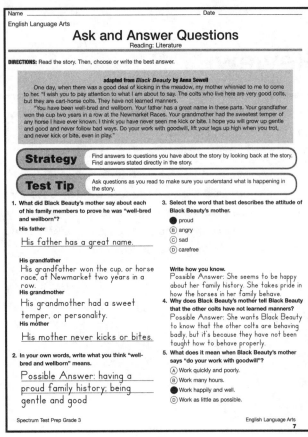

adapted from *Black Beauty* by Anna Sewell

One day, when there was a good deal of kicking in the meadow, my mother whinnied to me to come to her. "I wish you to pay attention to what I am about to say. The colts who live here are very good colts, but they are cart-horse colts. They have not learned manners.

"You have been well-bred and wellborn. Your father has a great name in these parts. Your grandfather won the cup two years in a row at the Newmarket Races. Your grandmother had the sweetest temper of any horse I have ever known. I think you have never seen me kick or bite. I hope you will grow up gentle and good and never follow bad ways. Do your work with goodwill, lift your legs up high when you trot, and never kick or bite, even in play."

Strategy Find answers to questions you have about the story by looking back at the story. Find answers stated directly in the story.

Test Tip Ask questions as you read to make sure you understand what is happening in the story.

1. What did Black Beauty's mother say about each of his family members to prove he was "well-bred and wellborn"?

His father

His father has a great name.

His grandfather

His grandfather won the cup, or horse race, at Newmarket two years in a row.

His grandmother

His grandmother had a sweet temper, or personality.

His mother

His mother never kicks or bites.

2. In your own words, write what you think "well-bred and wellborn" means.

Possible Answer: having a proud family history; being gentle and good

3. Select the word that best describes the attitude of Black Beauty's mother.

● proud
Ⓑ angry
Ⓒ sad
Ⓓ carefree

Write how you know.

Possible Answer: She seems to be happy about her family history. She takes pride in how the horses in her family behave.

4. Why does Black Beauty's mother tell Black Beauty that the other colts have not learned manners?

Possible Answer: She wants Black Beauty to know that the other colts are behaving badly, but it's because they have not been taught how to behave properly.

5. What does it mean when Black Beauty's mother says "do your work with goodwill"?

Ⓐ Work quickly and poorly.
Ⓑ Work many hours.
● Work happily and well.
Ⓓ Work as little as possible.

7

Ask and Answer Questions
Reading: Literature

DIRECTIONS: Read the story. Then, choose or write the best answer.

"The Fence" from *The Adventures of Tom Sawyer* by Mark Twain

Saturday morning was come, and all the summer world was bright and fresh, and brimming with life. There was a song in every heart . . . there was cheer in every face and a spring in every step. Tom appeared on the sidewalk with a bucket of whitewash and a long-handled brush. He surveyed the fence, and all gladness left him and a deep sadness settled down on his spirit. Thirty yards of board fence nine feet high. Life to him seemed hollow, and existence but a burden. Sighing, he dipped his brush and passed it along the topmost plank; repeated the operation; did it again; compared the small streak with the far-reaching continent of fence, and sat down on a tree-box discouraged.

Strategy Read the story carefully, paying attention to details. Use exactly what the story says to answer questions.

Test Tip Many stories have problems that the characters must solve. Look for details about a problem to help you understand the story.

1. What is the main problem in the story?

Ⓐ Tom did not know how to sing.
Ⓑ Tom needed another bucket.
Ⓒ Tom's brush was not long enough.
● Tom did not want to paint the fence.

2. What does the word "whitewash" mean?

Ⓐ soap and water
● white paint
Ⓒ cleaning solution
Ⓓ snow in the face

3. How were Tom's feelings about Saturday different from the feelings of those around him?

Possible Answer: Everybody else had a song in their heart, which meant they were happy. Tom was sad because he had to paint the huge fence.

4. Why do you think Tom sat down after painting just one small streak?

Ⓐ He was tired.
● He was overwhelmed.
Ⓒ He was lazy.
Ⓓ He was finished.

Choose two details from the story to support your answer to the question above.

Ⓐ "all gladness left him"
● "the far-reaching continent of fence"
● "Thirty yards of board fence"
Ⓓ "a deep sadness settled down"

5. Why is Tom "discouraged" at the end of the story?

Possible Answer: He has to work on a Saturday. He is upset that the fence is so long and so tall.

6. Which word in the story shows how Tom feels?

● sighing
Ⓑ cheer
Ⓒ surveyed
Ⓓ bright

Write how you know.

Possible Answer: The words **cheer** and **bright** are about being happy. The word **surveyed** is not a feeling, it is an action. When you sigh, you show sadness.

8

Recount Stories and Determine Theme
Reading: Literature

DIRECTIONS: Read the story. Then, choose or write the best answer.

The Fox and the Grapes by Aesop

One warm summer day, a fox was walking along when he saw a bunch of grapes on a vine above him. Cool, juicy grapes would taste so good. The more he thought about it, the more the fox wanted those grapes. He tried standing on his tiptoes. He tried jumping high in the air. He tried getting a running start before he jumped. But no matter what he tried, the fox could not reach the grapes. As he angrily walked away, the fox muttered, "They were probably sour anyway!" Moral: A person (or fox) sometimes pretends that he does not want something he cannot have.

Strategy Find the central message or main idea in a story by putting all of the details in the story together.

Test Tip Fables are stories that have lessons called *morals*. A moral is a lesson that teaches people how to act. The moral is the main idea of a fable.

1. These events from the story are out of order. Write the numbers 2, 3, 4, 5, 6, and 7 to retell the story in the correct order.

[1] One warm summer day, a fox was walking along.
[4] He tried standing on his tiptoes.
[6] No matter what he tried, the fox could not get the grapes.
[2] He saw a bunch of grapes on a vine above him.
[5] He tried jumping to get the grapes.
[3] The fox thought cool, juicy grapes would taste good.
[7] He walked away angrily.
[8] The fox muttered, "They were probably sour anyway!"

2. In your own words, state the lesson of this story.

Possible Answer: Sometimes, people say they don't want something, or something is probably bad, because they can't have it.

3. Which detail supports the story's lesson?

Ⓐ "fox wanted those grapes"
Ⓑ "he saw a bunch of grapes"
Ⓒ "grapes would taste so good"
● "They were probably sour"

4. Why did the fox say, "They were probably sour anyway"?

Ⓐ The grapes did not look ripe.
Ⓑ The grapes were all wrinkled.
● He couldn't reach them.
Ⓓ He tasted one, and it was sour.

5. In your own words, retell the fable.

Possible Answer: Fox saw grapes. He wanted to eat them. He tried to reach them many times. He could not reach them. He walked away angrily. He said the grapes were probably sour because he couldn't have them anyway.

9

Recount Stories and Determine Theme
Reading: Literature

DIRECTIONS: Read the story. Then, choose or write the best answer.

Why the Sun and the Moon Live in the Sky —Ghana folktale

Many, many years ago, the Sun and the Moon lived together on the earth. Water was their best friend, and they often came to see him. But Water never went to see the Sun and the Moon in their house. The Sun asked Water why he didn't visit. Water answered that he had too many friends and was afraid there would be no place for them in the Sun's house. So, the Sun built a very big house and then asked Water to come to him. Water came with all the fish and water animals. Soon, Water was up to the Sun's head and came higher and higher with all the fish and water animals. At last, Water was so high in the house that the Sun and the Moon went to the roof and sat there. Water soon came up onto the roof. What could the Sun and the Moon do? Where could they sit? They went up to the sky. They liked the place and began to live there.

Strategy Read the story and then retell the story in your own words. Retelling a story will help you know if you understand it or if you need to reread.

Test Tip Folktales are stories that tell how things began in nature. The main idea of a folktale is usually about how something began to happen.

1. These events from the story are out of order. Write the numbers 2, 3, 4, 5, 6, and 7 to retell the story in the correct order.

[1] Sun and Moon lived together on Earth.
[6] Water soon came up to the roof.
[3] Water did not think he would fit in the house.
[7] Sun and Moon went up to the sky.
[2] Water was their best friend, but he didn't visit.
[4] Sun built a very big house.
[5] Water came to visit with all his friends.
[8] Sun and Moon began to live in the sky.

2. What is the main idea of this folktale?

Ⓐ never invite Water to visit
Ⓑ Water has many friends
Ⓒ how fish and water animals live in oceans
● how the Sun and the Moon came to be in the sky

Write how you know.

Possible Answer: All of the details in the story tell about how the Sun and Moon ended up living in the sky.

3. Choose two details to support the main idea that you chose in question 2.

● "Water soon came up onto the roof"
Ⓑ "Water was their best friend"
Ⓒ "Water had too many friends"
● "Water was up to the Sun's head"

4. Write the detail that explains why Water would not fit in Sun and Moon's house.

Possible Answers: Water had too many friends. Water came with all the fish and water animals.

5. Retell the story in your own words.

Possible Answer: Sun and Moon wanted Water to visit them. Water was worried he would not fit in his house. Sun built a big house. Water came with all his friends. Water gets higher and higher. Sun and Moon have to move to the sky.

6. How do you know this is a folktale?

Possible Answer: The story is about how Sun and Moon begin living in the sky. A folktale tells about how things begin in nature.

10

Describe Characters and Their Actions
Reading: Literature

DIRECTIONS: Read the story. Then, choose or write the best answer.

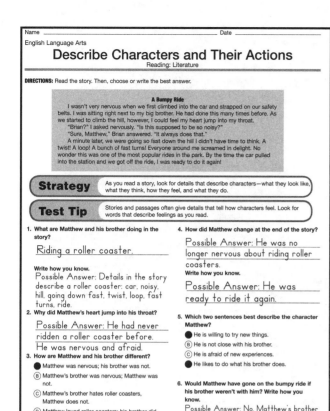

A Bumpy Ride

I wasn't very nervous when we first climbed into the car and strapped on our safety belts. I was sitting right next to my big brother. He had done this many times before. As we started to climb the hill, however, I could feel my heart jump into my throat.

"Brian?" I asked nervously. "Is this supposed to be so noisy?"

"Sure, Matthew," Brian answered. "It always does that."

A minute later, we were going so fast down the hill I didn't have time to think. A twist! A loop! A bunch of fast turns! Everyone around me screamed in delight. No wonder this was one of the most popular rides in the park. By the time the car pulled into the station and we got off the ride, I was ready to do it again!

Strategy As you read a story, look for details that describe characters—what they look like, what they think, how they feel, and what they do.

Test Tip Stories and passages often give details that tell how characters feel. Look for words that describe feelings as you read.

1. What are Matthew and his brother doing in the story?

Riding a roller coaster.

Write how you know.

Possible Answer: Details in the story describe a roller coaster: car, noisy, hill, going down fast, twist, loop, fast turns, ride.

2. Why did Matthew's heart jump into his throat?

Possible Answer: He had never ridden a roller coaster before. He was nervous and afraid.

3. How are Matthew and his brother different?

- (A) Matthew was nervous; his brother was not.
- (B) Matthew's brother was nervous; Matthew was not.
- (C) Matthew's brother hates roller coasters, Matthew does not.
- (D) Matthew loved roller coasters; his brother did not.

4. How did Matthew change at the end of the story?

Possible Answer: He was no longer nervous about riding roller coasters.

Write how you know.

Possible Answer: He was ready to ride it again.

5. Which two sentences best describe the character Matthew?

- ● He is willing to try new things.
- (B) He is not close with his brother.
- (C) He is afraid of new experiences.
- ● He likes to do what his brother does.

6. Would Matthew have gone on the bumpy ride if his brother weren't with him? Write how you know.

Possible Answer: No. Matthew's brother had ridden roller coasters many times before. This made Matthew less nervous.

Describe Characters and Their Actions
Reading: Literature

The Contest

Jin and Jo loved to enter contests. It did not matter what the prize was. Once, they wrote a poem for a magazine contest. They won a free copy of the magazine. Another time, they correctly guessed how many marbles were in a glass jar. They got to take all the marbles home with them. One morning, Jin was reading the Crunchy Munchies cereal box as he ate his breakfast.

"Jo," he said, "here's another contest! The first-place winner gets a bike. Second prize is a tent."

"Those are great prizes," said Jo. "How do we enter?"

The box said that the boys had to fill out a box top with their names and address. The more box tops they filled out, the better their chances for winning the drawing. Jin and Jo started eating Crunchy Munchies every morning. They also asked everyone they knew for cereal box tops. By the end of four weeks, Jin and Jo had sixteen box tops to send in for the drawing.

"I'm glad that's over," said Jin. "If I had to look at another box of that stuff, I don't know what I'd do." A few weeks passed. One day, the boys got a letter in the mail.

"Hooray! We've won third prize in the Crunchy Munchies contest!" Jo exclaimed. "I didn't even know there was a third prize."

Jin took the letter and started to read. His smile disappeared. "Oh, no!" he cried. "Third prize is a year's supply of Crunchy Munchies!"

Strategy Tell what characters do or what happens to them by looking for details in the story as you read.

Test Tip Characters have reasons for why they act the way they do. Look for details in the story that explain why characters think, say, or do something.

1. What is this story about?

- (A) two teachers who love cereal
- (B) two cereal makers who love contests
- (C) two sisters who play marbles
- ● two brothers who love contests

2. Why did Jin and Jo enter the Crunchy Munchies contest?

Possible Answer: They both loved to enter contests and did not care what the prize was.

3. What two actions do Jin and Jo take to try to win the contest?

- ● They ate Crunchy Munchies every morning.
- (B) They read the contest rules in a magazine.
- ● They asked everyone for cereal box tops.
- (D) They read the Crunchy Munchies cereal box.

4. What are Jin and Jo's feelings at the end of the story? Write how you know.

Possible Answer: They felt excited about winning third prize. (Jo exclaimed "Hooray!") They felt disappointed when they learned what the prize was. (Jin's smile disappeared.)

5. Why does Jin's smile disappear at the end of the story?

- (A) Jin and Jo can't figure out how to enter the contest.
- ● Jin and Jo ate so much cereal they don't want the prize.
- (C) Jin and Jo don't collect enough box tops to win.
- (D) Jin and Jo argue about who will get the prize.

6. Do you think Jin and Jo would have entered the contest if they knew what third prize would be? Provide details to explain your answer.

Possible Answer: Yes. They love the challenge of entering contests no matter what the prize might be.

Understand Literal and Nonliteral Language
Reading: Literature

DIRECTIONS: Read the poem. Then, choose or write the best answer.

My Bed Is a Boat *by Robert Louis Stevenson*

My bed is like a little boat;
    Nurse helps me in when I ¹embark;
She ²girds me in my sailor's coat
    And starts me in the dark.

At night, I go on board and say
    Good night to all my friends on shore;
I shut my eyes and sail away
    And see and hear no more.

And sometimes things to bed I take,
    As ³prudent sailors have to do;
Perhaps a slice of wedding-cake,
    Perhaps a toy or two.

All night across the dark we steer;
    But when the day returns at last
Safe in my room, beside the pier,
    I find my ⁴vessel fast.

¹ *embarks*—go on board a boat
² *girds*—dresses
³ *prudent*—careful
⁴ *vessel*—ship or large boat

Strategy As you read, determine the meaning of words and phrases in the story, poem, or passage.

Test Tip Nonliteral words and phrases can compare two things that are not usually compared. For example: *The dog was the size of a tank. His knee swelled up like a balloon after he fell.*

1. What does the speaker, or poem's narrator, compare his bed to?

a boat

Write two words or phrases from the poem that are details that support the comparison.

Possible Answers: embark, sailor's coat, shore, sail away, across the dark we steer, beside the pier, vessel

2. Read the lines from the poem below.

"I shut my eyes and sail away
And see and hear no more."

How do these lines give a detail about a bed like a boat?

- (A) Sailors see people when they sail.
- (B) Boats are silent on the water.
- ● The speaker is going to sleep.
- (D) It is night so there is nothing to see.

3. Does the speaker of the poem really "sail away"? Determine if this is literal or nonliteral language to explain your answer.

Possible answer: No. This is nonliteral language. The poet compares sleeping to sailing away.

4. Which sentence matches the meaning of the lines from the poem below?

"Nurse helps me in when I embark;
She girds me in my sailor's coat
And starts me in the dark."

- (A) The night nurse helps the speaker with his coat before taking him to the boat.
- ● The speaker's nanny helps him into bed, pulling the blankets over him.
- (C) They are at a hospital because the speaker is sick and needs care.
- (D) The nanny helps the speaker on the boat and sails with him.

Understand Literal and Nonliteral Language
Reading: Literature

DIRECTIONS: Read the story. Then, choose or write the best answer.

The Kite

It was the most tiresome kite in the world, always wagging its tail, shaking its ears, breaking its string, sitting down on the tops of houses, getting stuck in trees, entangled in hedges, flopping down on ponds, or lying flat on the grass, and refusing to rise higher than a yard from the ground.

I have often sat and thought about that kite, and wondered who its father and mother were. Perhaps they were very poor people, just made of newspaper and little bits of common string knotted together, obliged to fly day and night for a living, and never able to give any time to their children or to bring them up properly. It was pretty, for it had a snow-white face, and pink and white ears. And, with these, no one, let alone a kite, could help being pretty. But though the kite was pretty, it was not good, and it did not prosper. It came to a bad end, oh! a terrible end indeed. It stuck itself on a roof one day, a common red roof with a broken chimney and three tiles missing. It stuck itself there, and it would not move. The children tugged and pulled and coaxed and cried, but still it would not move. At last they fetched a ladder, and had nearly reached it when suddenly the kite started and flew away. Right away over the field and over the heath, and over the far, far woods, and it never came back again—never—never.

Dear, that is all. But I think sometimes that perhaps beyond the dark pines and the roaring sea the kite is flying still, on and on, farther and farther away, forever and forever.

Strategy Try using the dictionary definition of a word or phrase—the literal meaning—to see if that meaning makes sense. If it doesn't make sense, find a nonliteral meaning.

Test Tip Authors sometimes give human characteristics to a thing, idea, or animal. This is nonliteral language called *personification*. Look for details that give human qualities, such as feelings.

1. Which three details support the idea that the kite was "the most tiresome kite in the world"?

- ● shaking its ears
- ● refusing to rise higher
- (C) falling off of a roof
- ● wagging its tail
- (E) fetching a ladder
- (F) prospering and good

2. Does the kite actually do all of the things described in the first paragraph? Write how you know.

Possible Answer: No. The author is using nonliteral language. The author uses personification to describe the kite as moving on its own.

3. Describe what the kite looks like using details from the story.

Possible Answer: The kite is pretty. It has a white face and pink and white ears.

Which detail describing the kite is an example of nonliteral language? Write how you know.

pink and white ears; Kites do not have ears.

4. Why does the author wonder who the kite's parents are?

- (A) to thank them for the kite
- (B) to find more kites like this kite
- ● to understand the kite's bad behavior
- (D) to ask them to coax the kite off the roof

Identify Parts of Text
Reading: Literature

DIRECTIONS: Read the poem. Then, choose or write the best answer.

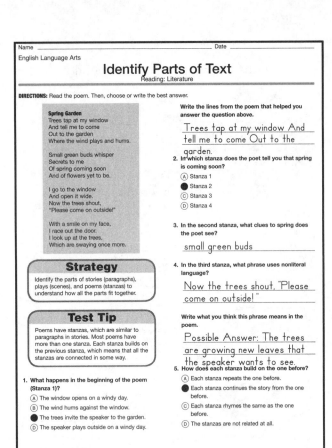

Spring Garden
Trees tap at my window
And tell me to come
Out to the garden
Where the wind plays and hums.

Small green buds whisper
Secrets to me
Of spring coming soon
And of flowers yet to be.

I go to the window
And open it wide.
Now the trees shout,
"Please come on outside!"

With a smile on my face,
I race out the door.
I look up at the trees,
Which are swaying once more.

Strategy
Identify the parts of stories (paragraphs), plays (scenes), and poems (stanzas) to understand how all the parts fit together.

Test Tip
Poems have stanzas, which are similar to paragraphs in stories. Most poems have more than one stanza. Each stanza builds on the previous stanza, which means that all the stanzas are connected in some way.

1. What happens in the beginning of the poem (Stanza 1)?
(A) The window opens on a windy day.
(B) The wind hums against the window.
● The trees invite the speaker to the garden.
(D) The speaker plays outside on a windy day.

Write the lines from the poem that helped you answer the question above.

Trees tap at my window And tell me to come Out to the garden.

2. In which stanza does the poet tell you that spring is coming soon?
(A) Stanza 1
● Stanza 2
(C) Stanza 3
(D) Stanza 4

3. In the second stanza, what clues to spring does the poet see?

small green buds

4. In the third stanza, what phrase uses nonliteral language?

Now the trees shout, "Please come on outside!"

Write what you think this phrase means in the poem.

Possible Answer: The trees are growing new leaves that the speaker wants to see.

5. How does each stanza build on the one before?
(A) Each stanza repeats the one before.
● Each stanza continues the story from the one before.
(C) Each stanza rhymes the same as the one before.
(D) The stanzas are not related at all.

Identify Parts of Text
Reading: Literature

DIRECTIONS: Read the poem. Then, choose or write the best answer.

"My Shadow" by Robert Louis Stevenson
I have a little shadow that goes in and out with me,
And what can be the use of him is more than I can see.
He is very, very like me, from the heels up to the head;
And I see him jump before me, when I jump into my bed.
The funniest thing about him is the way he likes to grow—
Not at all like proper children, which is always very slow;
For he sometimes shoots up taller, like an india-rubber ball,
And he sometimes gets so little that there's none of him at all.

He hasn't got a ¹notion of how children ought to play,
And can only make a fool of me in every sort of way.
He stays so close beside me, he's a coward you can see;
I'd ²think shame to stick to nurse as that shadow sticks to me!
One morning, very early, before the sun was up,
I ˈrose and found the shining dew on every buttercup;
But my lazy little shadow, like an ³arrant sleepy head,
Had stayed at home behind me and was fast asleep in bed.

¹ notion—idea, understanding
² think shame to stick to nurse—be embarrassed to stay close to my nanny
³ arrant—complete, extreme

Strategy
Figure out the meaning of the other stanzas in a poem by using what you know about the first stanza.

Test Tip
Remember that poems have stanzas that build on each other. Poems are about one topic or theme, just like stories. Think about what a poem is mainly about to understand it better.

1. What is the poet describing?
(A) playing
● his shadow
(C) sleeping
(D) morning

2. Write one line that tells you what the poem is about.
Possible Answer: I have a little shadow that goes in and out with me.

3. Which sentence best describes how the two stanzas build on each other?
(A) Stanza 1 describes why shadows exist. Stanza 2 continues that explanation.
(B) Stanza 1 is about the speaker's fear of shadows. Stanza 2 gives reasons for that fear.
(C) Stanza 1 explains what a shadow is. Stanza 2 explains what shadows do.
● Stanza 1 tells about how the shadow looks. Stanza 2 tells how the shadow acts.

4. Write two lines from the poem that show that the speaker is bothered by his shadow.

Possible Answers: what can be the use of him is more than I can see; He hasn't got a notion of how children ought to play, And can only make a fool of me in every sort of way.

Identify Points of View
Reading: Literature

DIRECTIONS: Read each paragraph. Then, choose or write the best answer.

A Sad Tale
A. I felt sorry for Jason when I saw him come in this morning. He looked so sad. I could tell he had a hard time focusing in class. When it was finally time for recess, I asked him to stay behind. Then, he told me his problem. With one quick phone call, the problem was solved.

B. I was in such a rush this morning that I forgot the permission form for the school field trip. The class was going to a museum that had a life-sized dinosaur skeleton. Mom had even reminded me that today was the last day to turn it in. And now I would miss it! At recess, Ms. Warner asked me what was wrong. Then, she made a phone call, and Mom soon brought the form to school.

C. As soon as Jason left for the bus, I saw his permission form sitting on the counter. I had planned to bring it to school anyway. I couldn't let Jason miss a chance to see dinosaurs—they are his favorite things! I was glad that Ms. Warner called and told Jason I was on my way. Jason was so happy that he would be able to go to the dinosaur museum!

Strategy
As you read, identify the narrator, or who is telling the story, and note what he or she knows about characters and what is happening to them in the story.

Test Tip
A narrator may be a character in the story or the voice of someone outside the story. Point of view describes what characters and narrators know, think, or feel. First-person point of view is when the narrator is a character in the story. First-person point of view uses the word I. Narrators also share their thoughts and feelings.

1. Write who narrates, or tells the story, in each paragraph.
Paragraph A: _Jason's teacher, Ms. Warner_
Paragraph B: _Jason_
Paragraph C: _Jason's mom_

Write one detail you used to determine the narrators for each paragraph.
Paragraph A: _Possible Answer: She notices he is sad and can't focus in class._
Paragraph B: _Possible Answer: He shares his problem, or why he is sad._
Paragraph C: _Possible Answer: She sees his permission slip on the counter._

2. What is the problem that each narrator wants to solve in each paragraph?
Paragraph A: _Ms. Warner wants to know why Jason is sad and help him._
Paragraph B: _Jason forgot his permission form and it's the last day to turn it in._
Paragraph C: _Jason's mom sees Jason forgot the form._

3. Which narrator does not know the reason that Jason is sad?

Jason's teacher, Ms. Warner

Explain why the narrator does not know.
Possible Answer: Jason and his mom know what Jason's problem is, so they know why he is sad. Mrs. Warner only knows what she sees or what Jason tells her.

4. Which point of view is used in each paragraph?

first person

Write how you know.
Possible Answers: All of the narrators are characters in the story. They use the word I. They share their thoughts.

Identify Points of View
Reading: Literature

DIRECTIONS: Read the story. Then, choose or write the best answer.

Lunch Guests
It was a sunny spring day. Kaye and her friend, Tasha, were walking in the woods. As they walked, they noticed many squirrels ahead of them running in the same direction.
"Let's follow them and see where they are going," Kaye said.
"Great idea!" exclaimed Tasha, and the two girls raced ahead.
Soon, they came to a large clearing in the forest. There were hundreds and hundreds of squirrels. There were more squirrels than either girl had ever seen. They stared in amazement at the scene before them. Then, a plump gray squirrel with a fluffy tail skittered over to them and said politely, "Would you care to join us for lunch?"
Kaye and Tasha were stunned into silence. But after a moment, they looked at each other, shrugged, and said, "Why not?" They both liked nuts.

Strategy
As you read a story, find clues about the point of view by identifying the narrator.

Test Tip
A narrator may be a character in the story (first-person point of view) or the voice of someone who is not part of the story (third-person point of view). The narrator tells what happens and may tell what some or all of the characters think or feel.

1. From whose point of view is this story told?
(A) Kaye's first-person point of view
(B) Tasha's point of view
(C) the squirrel's point of view
● a narrator's third-person point of view

2. Which two things does the story's narrator know?
● the setting of the story
● what Tasha and Kaye think
(C) the squirrels' thoughts
(D) why the girls are friends

3. Rewrite the first paragraph from Kaye's point of view.
Possible Answer: It was a sunny spring day. My friend, Tasha, and I were walking in the woods. As we walked, we noticed many squirrels ahead of us running in the same direction.

4. How did Kaye and Tasha feel about a talking squirrel inviting them to lunch?
(A) scared
(B) angry
● stunned
(D) jealous

Write how you know.
Possible Answer: The narrator says that the girls were stunned into silence.

5. What would be different about the story if it were written in first-person point of view?
Possible Answer: The word I would be used. The narrator would be a character in the story.

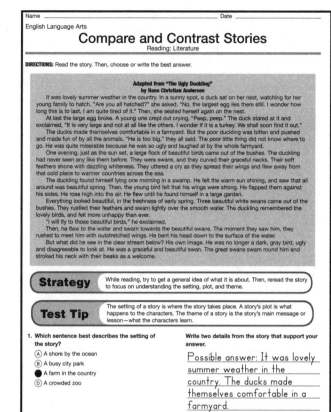

Name ______________________ Date ______________

English Language Arts

Compare and Contrast Stories

Reading: Literature

DIRECTIONS: Read the story. Then, choose or write the best answer.

Adapted from "The Ugly Duckling"
by Hans Christian Andersen

It was lovely summer weather in the country. In a sunny spot, a duck sat on her nest, watching for her young family to hatch. "Are you all hatched?" she asked. "No, the largest egg lies there still. I wonder how long this is to last, I am quite tired of it." Then, she seated herself again on the nest.

At last the large egg broke. A young one crept out crying, "Peep, peep." The duck stared at it and exclaimed, "It is very large and not at all like the others. I wonder if it is a turkey. We shall soon find it out."

The ducks made themselves comfortable in a farmyard. But the poor duckling was bitten and pushed and made fun of by all the animals. "He is too big," they all said. The poor little thing did not know where to go. He was quite miserable because he was so ugly and laughed at by the whole farmyard.

One evening, just as the sun set, a large flock of beautiful birds came out of the bushes. The duckling had never seen any like them before. They were swans, and they curved their graceful necks. Their soft feathers shone with dazzling whiteness. They uttered a cry as they spread their wings and flew away from that cold place to warmer countries across the sea.

The duckling found himself lying one morning in a swamp. He felt the warm sun shining, and saw that all around was beautiful spring. Then, the young bird felt that his wings were strong. He flapped them against his sides. He rose high into the air. He flew until he found himself in a large garden.

Everything looked beautiful, in the freshness of early spring. Three beautiful white swans came out of the bushes. They rustled their feathers and swam lightly over the smooth water. The duckling remembered the lovely birds, and felt more unhappy than ever.

"I will fly to those beautiful birds," he exclaimed.

Then, he flew to the water and swam towards the beautiful swans. The moment they saw him, they rushed to meet him with outstretched wings. He bent his head down to the surface of the water.

But what did he see in the clear stream below? His own image. He was no longer a dark, gray bird, ugly and disagreeable to look at. He was a graceful and beautiful swan. The great swans swam round him and stroked his neck with their beaks as a welcome.

Strategy While reading, try to get a general idea of what it is about. Then, reread the story to focus on understanding the setting, plot, and theme.

Test Tip The setting of a story is where the story takes place. A story's plot is what happens to the characters. The theme of a story is the story's main message or lesson—what the characters learn.

1. Which sentence best describes the setting of the story?

- Ⓐ A shore by the ocean
- Ⓑ A busy city park
- ● A farm in the country
- Ⓓ A crowded zoo

Write two details from the story that support your answer.

Possible answer: It was lovely summer weather in the country. The ducks made themselves comfortable in a farmyard.

Spectrum Test Prep Grade 3 English Language Arts 19

19

Name ______________________ Date ______________

English Language Arts

Compare and Contrast Stories

Reading: Literature

DIRECTIONS: Determine the problem a character must solve or overcome by identifying the plot of a story.

Strategy Determine the problem a character must solve or overcome by identifying the plot of a story.

Test Tip Remember that a theme of a story is not the story's topic. A theme is an overall idea or message the story gives to readers.

2. Who is the main character in this story?

- ● A large duckling
- Ⓑ A beautiful tree
- Ⓒ A flock of swans
- Ⓓ A family of ducks

3. Write the problem that the biggest duckling needed to solve.

Possible Answer: The biggest duckling did not look like the other ducklings. He was big and gray. Everyone thought he was ugly.

4. Which two ways was the ugly duckling able to solve his problem?

- Ⓐ He chose to run away, flying to another farmyard.
- ● He decided to join the swans, swimming to them.
- ● He grew into a graceful, white swan as time passed.
- Ⓓ He began to tease the other ducklings.

5. Write a reason for how the swans behaved when the ugly duckling swam for them. Use details about the story's plot, or what happens to the characters in the story.

Possible Answer: The swans rushed to meet the ugly duckling. They were happy to see him. They knew he was a swan, too.

6. What is the best theme for the story?

- Ⓐ Trying to change or grow for the better will never work.
- Ⓑ All ugly creatures will grow up to be beautiful and loved.
- Ⓒ Try not to look or act different from others or you will be teased.
- ● It is okay to look different, because everyone is beautiful.

Write how you know.

Possible Answer: The ugly duckling didn't deserve to be teased for looking different. He was beautiful in the end.

7. What do you think the ugly duckling learned in the story?

Possible Answer: Don't let others tease you for being different. Find others who like you for who you are.

English Language Arts 20 Spectrum Test Prep Grade 3

20

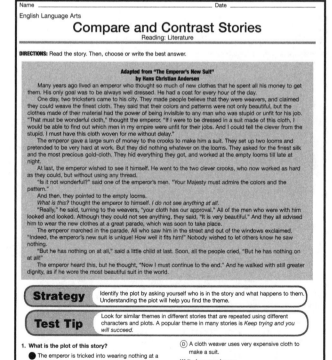

Name ______________________ Date ______________

English Language Arts

Compare and Contrast Stories

Reading: Literature

DIRECTIONS: Read the story. Then, choose or write the best answer.

Adapted from "The Emperor's New Suit"
by Hans Christian Andersen

Many years ago lived an emperor who thought so much of new clothes that he spent all his money to get them. His only goal was to be always well dressed. He had a coat for every hour of the day.

One day, two tricksters came to his city. They made people believe that they were weavers, and claimed they could weave the finest cloth. They said that their colors and patterns were not only beautiful, but the clothes made of their material had the power of being invisible to any man who was stupid or unfit for his job. "That must be wonderful cloth," thought the emperor. "If I were to be dressed in a suit made of this cloth, I would be able to find out which men in my empire were unfit for their jobs. And I could tell the clever from the stupid. I must have this cloth woven for me without delay."

The emperor gave a large sum of money to the crooks to make him a suit. They set up two looms and pretended to be very hard at work. But they did nothing whatever on the looms. They asked for the finest silk and the most precious gold-cloth. They hid everything they got, and worked at the empty looms till late at night.

At last, the emperor wished to see it himself. He went to the two clever crooks, who now worked as hard as they could, but without using any thread.

"Is it not wonderful?" said one of the emperor's men. "Your Majesty must admire the colors and the pattern."

And then, they pointed to the empty looms.

What is this? thought the emperor to himself. *I do not see anything at all.*

"Really," he said, turning to the weavers, "your cloth has our approval." All of the men who were with him looked and looked. Although they could not see anything, they said, "It is very beautiful." And they all advised him to wear the new clothes at a great parade, which was soon to take place.

The emperor marched in the parade. All who saw him in the street and out of the windows exclaimed, "Indeed, the emperor's new suit is unique! How well it fits him!" Nobody wished to let others know he saw nothing.

"But he has nothing on at all," said a little child at last. Soon, all the people cried, "But he has nothing on at all!"

The emperor heard this, but he thought, "Now I must continue to the end." And he walked with still greater dignity, as if he wore the most beautiful suit in the world.

Strategy Identify the plot by asking yourself who is in the story and what happens to them. Understanding the plot will help you find the theme.

Test Tip Look for similar themes in different stories that are repeated using different characters and plots. A popular theme in many stories is *Keep trying and you will succeed.*

1. What is the plot of this story?

- ● The emperor is tricked into wearing nothing at a parade.
- Ⓑ The tricksters helped the emperor fire people who were unfit.
- Ⓒ The people prepared for a parade by buying clothes.
- Ⓓ A cloth weaver uses very expensive cloth to make a suit.

Write how you know.

Possible Answer: The story calls the weavers "tricksters" and says that they pretended to weave an invisible suit. The emperor won't admit the suit isn't real because he doesn't want to be seen as stupid.

Spectrum Test Prep Grade 3 English Language Arts 21

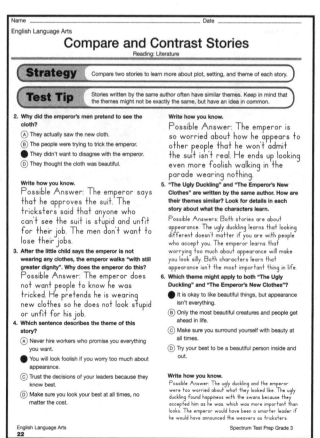

21

Name ______________________ Date ______________

English Language Arts

Compare and Contrast Stories

Reading: Literature

Strategy Compare two stories to learn more about plot, setting, and theme of each story.

Test Tip Stories written by the same author often have similar themes. Keep in mind that the themes might not be exactly the same, but have an idea in common.

2. Why did the emperor's men pretend to see the cloth?

- Ⓐ They actually saw the new cloth.
- Ⓑ The people were trying to trick the emperor.
- ● They didn't want to disagree with the emperor.
- Ⓓ They thought the cloth was beautiful.

Write how you know.

Possible Answer: The emperor says that he approves the suit. The tricksters said that anyone who can't see the suit is stupid and unfit for their job. The men don't want to lose their jobs.

3. After the little child says the emperor is not wearing any clothes, the emperor walks "with still greater dignity". Why does the emperor do this?

Possible Answer: The emperor does not want people to know he was tricked. He pretends he is wearing new clothes so he does not look stupid or unfit for his job.

4. Which sentence describes the theme of this story?

- Ⓐ Never hire workers who promise you everything you want.
- ● You will look foolish if you worry too much about appearance.
- Ⓒ Trust the decisions of your leaders because they know best.
- Ⓓ Make sure you look your best at all times, no matter the cost.

Write how you know.

Possible Answer: The emperor is so worried about how he appears to other people that he won't admit the suit isn't real. He ends up looking even more foolish walking in the parade wearing nothing.

5. "The Ugly Duckling" and "The Emperor's New Clothes" are written by the same author. How are their themes similar? Look for details in each story about what the characters learn.

Possible Answers: Both stories are about appearance. The ugly duckling learns that looking different doesn't matter if you are with people who accept you. The emperor learns that worrying too much about appearance will make you look silly. Both characters learn that appearance isn't the most important thing in life.

6. Which theme might apply to both "The Ugly Duckling" and "The Emperor's New Clothes"?

- ● It is okay to like beautiful things, but appearance isn't everything.
- Ⓑ Only the most beautiful creatures and people get ahead in life.
- Ⓒ Make sure you surround yourself with beauty at all times.
- Ⓓ Try your best to be a beautiful person inside and out.

Write how you know.

Possible Answer: The ugly duckling and the emperor were too worried about what they looked like. The ugly duckling found happiness with the swans because they accepted him as he was, which was more important than looks. The emperor would have been a smarter leader if he would have announced the weavers as tricksters.

English Language Arts 22 Spectrum Test Prep Grade 3

22

Name _____ Date _____

English Language Arts

Demonstrate Understanding of a Text
Reading: Informational Text

DIRECTIONS: Read the passage. Then, choose or write the best answer.

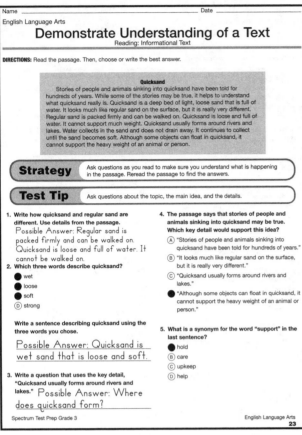

Quicksand

Stories of people and animals sinking into quicksand have been told for hundreds of years. While some of the stories may be true, it helps to understand what quicksand really is. Quicksand is a deep bed of light, loose sand that is full of water. It looks much like regular sand on the surface, but it is really very different. Regular sand is packed firmly and can be walked on. Quicksand is loose and full of water. It cannot support much weight. Quicksand usually forms around rivers and lakes. Water collects in the sand and does not drain away. It continues to collect until the sand becomes soft. Although some objects can float in quicksand, it cannot support the heavy weight of an animal or person.

Strategy Ask questions as you read to make sure you understand what is happening in the passage. Reread the passage to find the answers.

Test Tip Ask questions about the topic, the main idea, and the details.

1. Write how quicksand and regular sand are different. Use details from the passage.
Possible Answer: Regular sand is packed firmly and can be walked on. Quicksand is loose and full of water. It cannot be walked on.

2. Which three words describe quicksand?
● wet
● loose
● soft
Ⓓ strong

Write a sentence describing quicksand using the three words you chose.
Possible Answer: Quicksand is wet sand that is loose and soft.

3. Write a question that uses the key detail, "Quicksand usually forms around rivers and lakes." Possible Answer: Where does quicksand form?

4. The passage says that stories of people and animals sinking into quicksand may be true. Which key detail would support this idea?
Ⓐ "Stories of people and animals sinking into quicksand have been told for hundreds of years."
Ⓑ "It looks much like regular sand on the surface, but it is really very different."
Ⓒ "Quicksand usually forms around rivers and lakes."
● "Although some objects can float in quicksand, it cannot support the heavy weight of an animal or person."

5. What is a synonym for the word "support" in the last sentence?
● hold
Ⓑ care
Ⓒ upkeep
Ⓓ help

Spectrum Test Prep Grade 3

English Language Arts
23

23

Name _____ Date _____

English Language Arts

Demonstrate Understanding of a Text
Reading: Informational Text

DIRECTIONS: Read the passage. Then, choose or write the best answer.

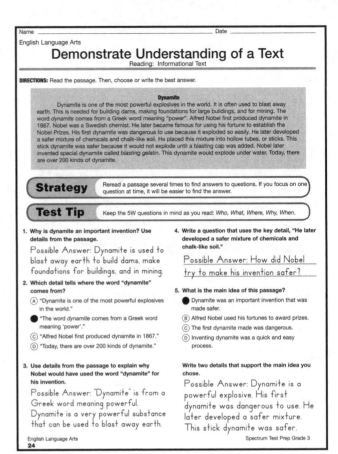

Dynamite

Dynamite is one of the most powerful explosives in the world. It is often used to blast away earth. This is needed for building dams, making foundations for large buildings, and for mining. The word *dynamite* comes from a Greek word meaning "power". Alfred Nobel first produced dynamite in 1867. Nobel was a Swedish chemist. He later became famous for using his fortune to establish the Nobel Prizes. His first dynamite was dangerous to use because it exploded so easily. He later developed a safer mixture of chemicals and chalk-like soil. He placed this mixture into hollow tubes, or sticks. This stick dynamite was safer because it would not explode until a blasting cap was added. Nobel later invented special dynamite called *blasting gelatin*. This dynamite would explode under water. Today, there are over 200 kinds of dynamite.

Strategy Reread a passage several times to find answers to questions. If you focus on one question at time, it will be easier to find the answer.

Test Tip Keep the 5W questions in mind as you read: *Who, What, Where, Why, When.*

1. Why is dynamite an important invention? Use details from the passage.
Possible Answer: Dynamite is used to blast away earth to build dams, make foundations for buildings, and in mining.

2. Which detail tells where the word "dynamite" comes from?
Ⓐ "Dynamite is one of the most powerful explosives in the world."
● "The word *dynamite* comes from a Greek word meaning 'power'."
Ⓒ "Alfred Nobel first produced dynamite in 1867."
Ⓓ "Today, there are over 200 kinds of dynamite."

3. Use details from the passage to explain why Nobel would have used the word "dynamite" for his invention.
Possible Answer: "Dynamite" is from a Greek word meaning powerful. Dynamite is a very powerful substance that can be used to blast away earth.

4. Write a question that uses the key detail, "He later developed a safer mixture of chemicals and chalk-like soil."
Possible Answer: How did Nobel try to make his invention safer?

5. What is the main idea of this passage?
● Dynamite was an important invention that was made safer.
Ⓑ Alfred Nobel used his fortunes to award prizes.
Ⓒ The first dynamite made was dangerous.
Ⓓ Inventing dynamite was a quick and easy process.

Write two details that support the main idea you chose.
Possible Answer: Dynamite is a powerful explosive. His first dynamite was dangerous to use. He later developed a safer mixture. This stick dynamite was safer.

English Language Arts
24

Spectrum Test Prep Grade 3

24

Name _____ Date _____

English Language Arts

Determine Main Idea
Reading: Informational Text

DIRECTIONS: Read the passage. Then, choose or write the best answer.

Marie Curie

One of the greatest scientists of all time is Marie Curie. Marie Curie was born in Poland in 1867. She studied at a university in Paris and lived in France for most of her adult life. Along with her husband, she studied radioactivity. Radioactivity is what happens to atoms when they quickly break down. Radiation, the energy sent out by the atom as it breaks down, can be very dangerous to people and animals. Marie Curie was awarded the Nobel Prize in 1911 for her work discovering radium and polonium, two radioactive elements. Some medical advances are based on the research of the Marie Curie and her husband. They include the X-ray and the use of radiation to treat cancer.
The Curies were both generous people. Even though they were poor for most of their lives, they did not patent, or keep the rights to, any of their discoveries. They wanted everyone to benefit from their research. Marie Curie died in 1934. The world should not forget her.

Strategy Use the details in a passage to identify the main idea. Put all of the details together and see what idea they are mostly about.

Test Tip Keep the 5W questions in mind as you read: *Who, What, Where, Why, When.* Finding answers to these questions will help you find the main idea.

1. Write three details from the passage that support the main idea below.

Main Idea	One of the greatest scientists of all time is Marie Curie.
Detail 1:	Marie Curie was awarded the Nobel Prize in chemistry in 1911 for her work discovering radium and polonium.
Detail 2:	Some medical advances are based on the research of the Curies.
Detail 3:	They wanted everyone to benefit from their research.

2. Which key details support the idea that the Curies were generous? Choose all that apply.
Ⓐ They were poor for most of their lives.
● They did not keep the rights to their discoveries.
● They wanted everyone to have their research.
Ⓓ They studied radioactivity and chemistry.

3. What is radioactivity? Use details from the passage.
Radioactivity is what happens to atoms when they quickly break down. The energy sent out is dangerous to people and animals.

4. What modern technologies may not exist if it weren't for Marie Curie and her husband? Choose all that apply.
Ⓐ cars
● X-ray
Ⓒ vaccines
● cancer treatments

5. How does the author of the passage feel about Marie Curie? Use details from the passage.
The author admires and respects Marie Curie. The author notes all of Curie's discoveries and says that we should not forget her.

Spectrum Test Prep Grade 3

English Language Arts
25

25

Name _____ Date _____

English Language Arts

Determine Main Idea
Reading: Informational Text

DIRECTIONS: Read each passage carefully. Then, choose the best answer for the question.

Insects in Winter

In the summertime, insects can be seen buzzing and fluttering around us. But as winter's cold weather begins, the insects seem to disappear. Do you know where they go? Many insects find a warm place to spend the winter.
Ants try to dig deep into the ground. Some beetles stack up in piles under rocks or dead leaves. Female grasshoppers don't even stay around for winter. In the fall, they lay their eggs and die. The eggs hatch in the spring.
Bees also try to protect themselves from the winter cold. Honeybees gather in a ball in the middle of their hive. The bees stay in this tight ball trying to stay warm. Winter is very hard for insects, but each spring the survivors come out and the buzzing and fluttering begins again.

Strategy Look for at least two details that support the main idea you have found. If you can't find supporting details, find a new main idea.

Test Tip Remember that every main idea has details that support it. Reread the passage and look for details that lead to a main idea.

1. Use the passage to fill in the main idea below. Fill in the rest of the ovals with supporting details.

Many insects find a **warm** place to spend the **winter**.

- Ants dig into the ground.
- Female grasshoppers lay their eggs and die.
- Bees gather in the middle of their hive.

2. Why doesn't the author mention how animals survive in the winter? Use the main idea to answer.
Possible Answer: The main idea is about how insects survive in winter. Animals are not part of the main idea or the topic.

3. How are bees and beetles similar in the way they try to protect themselves in the winter?
Possible Answer: Both bees and beetles gather together to keep warm in winter. Beetles stack up in piles, while bees cluster together in a ball.

4. How do the details support the main idea?
Ⓐ The details are about how animals hibernate.
Ⓑ The details are about the different kinds of insects.
● The details are about what insects do to survive winter.
Ⓓ The details are about insects that die in the winter.

English Language Arts
26

Spectrum Test Prep Grade 3

26

Describe Relationships in Texts
Reading: Informational Text

DIRECTIONS: Read the passage. Then, choose or write the best answer.

The Great Ice Age

Long ago, the climate of the earth began to cool. As the temperature dropped, giant sheets of ice, called *glaciers*, moved across the land. As time went on, snow and ice covered many forests and grasslands. Some plants and animals could not survive the changes in the climate. Other animals moved to warmer land. But some animals were able to adapt. They learned to live with the cold and snowy weather because they changed. Finally, the earth's temperature began to rise. The ice and snow began to melt. Today, the land at the North and South Poles is a reminder of the Great Ice Age.

Strategy — List all of the ideas or events in a passage. Then, determine how each idea or event is connected, or fits together in the passage.

Test Tip — Authors use words to connect ideas. Sometimes, authors use words about time (*first, next, last*) or about cause and effect (*because, then, so*).

1. Use the graphic organizer to list the events of the Great Ice Age in order. Use details from the passage.

| 1. The climate of the earth began to cool. |
| 2. Gigantic sheets of ice moved across the land. |
| 3. Snow and ice covered forests and grasslands. |
| 4. Many plants and animals died. |
| 5. Some animals moved to warmer places. |
| 6. Some animals adapted. |
| 7. The earth's temperature began to rise. |
| 8. Ice and snow began to melt. |

2. Write at least two words that connect ideas. Look for words about time or cause and effect.

Possible Answers: Long ago, As, As time went on, because, Finally, Today

3. According to the passage, what does "glaciers" mean?

giant sheets of ice

4. Why did the author say that the land at the North and South Poles is a reminder of the Great Ice Age?

Possible Answer: The land at the North and South Poles is a reminder of the Great Ice Age because it is very cold and icy, and few plants or animals can survive those areas.

5. What happened to plants and animals that could not adapt to or escape the new climate?

They died.

6. During the Great Ice Age, did snow and ice cover all of the earth? Explain, using details from the passage.

Possible Answer: No, the passage stated that snow and ice covered many but not all forests and grasslands and that some animals moved to warmer land.

Spectrum Test Prep Grade 3

English Language Arts 27

27

Describe Relationships in Texts
Reading: Informational Text

DIRECTIONS: Read the passage. Then, choose or write the best answer.

Tornadoes and Hurricanes

It is easy to see why people get hurricanes and tornadoes mixed up. Both are strong storms that have high winds. They both can cause a large amount of damage. Hurricanes and tornadoes can both appear in either the Northern or Southern hemispheres. Hurricanes and tornadoes rotate differently in each hemisphere. South of the equator, they rotate clockwise. North of the equator, they rotate counterclockwise. However, they are different in some ways.

Tornadoes originate, or begin, from strong thunderstorms. They extend down to the ground. They are funnel-shaped and are very hard to predict. In the United States, there are about 1,000 tornadoes reported each year. Tornadoes can have wind speeds up to 300 miles per hour. Because of this high wind, these storms can pull trees out of the ground and send cars flying hundreds of yards into the air. A tornado usually moves about 30 miles per hour. Tornadoes can last several seconds or over an hour.

Hurricanes, on the other hand, form over the ocean. A hurricane can be up to 600 miles across and make winds up to 200 miles per hour. Each hurricane usually lasts for over a week. They move 10 to 20 miles per hour. When a hurricane reaches land, it can cause huge storm surges with heavy rains. A storm surge is when a storm along a coastline causes the tide to rise to very high levels. This causes flooding. Hurricanes can be predicted and tracked.

While both tornadoes and hurricanes are large storms that can cause major damage, they each have their own features.

Strategy — Compare two or more ideas to see how they are connected. Look for how an idea builds on the previous idea.

Test Tip — In addition to words about time or about cause and effect, authors also describe ideas by comparing and contrasting them. Look for words such as *however, on the other hand,* or *both*.

1. How are the ideas in this passage connected?
   - (A) sequence of events
   - (B) cause and effect
   - ● compare and contrast
   - (D) time order

   Which words does the author use to connect ideas?

   Both, However, Because, on the other hand

2. According to the passage, what causes a tornado?
   - (A) a storm over the ocean
   - (B) high winds
   - (C) storm surges
   - ● strong thunderstorms

3. Complete the Venn diagram about tornadoes and hurricanes. Use details from the passage.

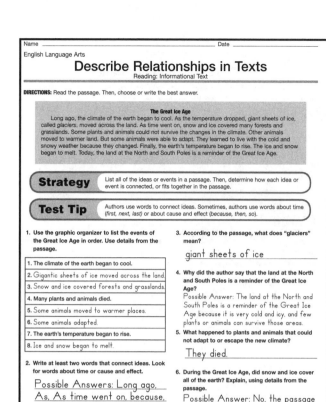

Tornadoes: form from thunderstorms, 300 mph winds, funnel-shaped, form over land, last seconds to over an hour, hard to predict

Both: strong storms, cause damage, form in both hemispheres

Hurricanes: form over oceans, cause flooding, last weeks, travel 10–20 mph

4. Why does the author discuss two ideas—hurricanes and tornadoes? Explain how the two ideas are connected.

Possible Answer: Both are strong storms that cause a lot of damage. The author discusses both ideas to compare and contrast each kind of storm.

English Language Arts 28

Spectrum Test Prep Grade 3

28

Describe Connections
Reading: Informational Text

DIRECTIONS: Read the passage. Then, choose or write the best answer.

Jobs During World War II

World War II changed the way people of the United States lived and worked. On December 7, 1941, the Japanese attacked Pearl Harbor, Hawaii. Because of this, the United States entered World War II. The shift in the way Americans lived and worked seemed to change overnight.

Before World War II, the United States was recovering from the Great Depression. The Great Depression was a time when people had very little money. Many people were out of work. The United States government had been focusing on the problems here rather than problems in other countries. Most workers in the United States were men. Women usually took care of children and the home.

After the attack on Pearl Harbor, thousands of men joined the armed forces to fight the war. Women had to take jobs to help win the war. Men had performed these jobs. Women became welders, electricians, and factory workers. The number of women in the work place almost doubled during this time. Because more Americans had jobs during the war, people's lives began to improve.

Strategy — Identify clue words in sentences and paragraphs to understand how an author connects sentences and paragraphs.

Test Tip — An author may write sentences that compare, show cause and effect, or sequence. Words such as *before, after,* and *during* show sequence (time) and show comparison (something happened before or after an event).

1. What is the author's opinion about the effect of World War II on the people of the United States?
   - (A) The author thinks the war was bad for the people of the United States.
   - ● The author thinks the war was good for the people of the United States.
   - (C) The author thinks the war had no effect on the people of the United States.
   - (D) The author thinks women should not have gone to work during the war.

2. What caused the United States to enter the war?

   the Japanese attack on Pearl Harbor

   Write the key detail that helped you answer the question.

   Because of this, the United States entered World War II.

3. Why did more women go to work after December of 1941?
   - (A) They were tired of not earning their own money.
   - (B) The government wanted them to join the armed forces.
   - ● There were not enough men at home to do the work.
   - (D) They were tired of taking care of children and homes.

4. The main idea of this passage is, "World War II changed the way people of the United States lived and worked." Write three details to support this main idea.

   Possible Answer: men went to fight the war; women started working; people had more money

5. What is your opinion on the effect of World War II on the people of the United States?

   Possible Answer: I agree with the author. Even though the war was hard, more Americans had jobs during the war.

Spectrum Test Prep Grade 3

English Language Arts 29

29

Describe Connections
Reading: Informational Text

DIRECTIONS: Read the passage. Then, choose or write the best answer.

How to Make a Terrarium

A terrarium is a miniature garden. It grows inside a covered glass or plastic container. A terrarium can easily be made out of common materials.

To make a terrarium, you first need to gather some supplies. You will need a 2-liter soda bottle, a marker, a sharp pair of scissors, 2 cups of soil, some seeds, a few rocks, and a spray bottle of water.

First, wash out the soda bottle and remove the label. Then, use the marker to draw a line around the bottle about $\frac{1}{4}$ of the way from the bottom. Use the sharp scissors to cut along the line so that the bottle is in two pieces. Be very careful doing this step!

After you have prepared the bottle, place the rocks in the bottom of the bottle. You can add peat moss, too. This will give the roots more room to breathe. Lightly pour the soil over the rocks and peat moss. Place the seeds in the soil. Follow the directions on the seed packet to know how deep to plant them.

Finally, lightly spray the soil with water. Slide the top of the bottle down over the bottom so that it overlaps. Keep the cap on. This will keep moisture in the bottle. Place your terrarium in the sun and watch your plants grow!

Your plants will grow nicely in the terrarium with very little work. If the soil starts to look dry, simply open the cap and spray in a little bit of water.

Strategy — As you read a how-to passage, find details that tell when each step is done and how. The order of steps connects ideas.

Test Tip — How-to passages tell how to do something. Look for words such as *first, next, then, last,* and *finally*.

1. How are the paragraphs in this passage connected?
   - (A) cause and effect
   - ● sequence
   - (C) compare and contrast
   - (D) facts and details

2. Look at your answer to the previous question. Why did the author choose to write the passage this way?

   Possible Answer: The author is giving instructions on how to do something. You do the steps in a particular order. Sequence is time order.

3. Which words does the author use to show how ideas are connected?

   Possible Answer: first, then, after, finally

4. Why does the author tell you to keep the top on the bottle?

   to keep the moisture in

5. What is the purpose of putting rocks and peat moss under the soil?
   - (A) to make the level higher
   - (B) to hold the roots in place
   - (C) to look pretty
   - ● to give the roots room to breathe

6. What would happen if the author didn't connect the sentences and paragraphs in this passage? Reread the passage and think about the information given.

   Possible Answer: Readers wouldn't know the correct order of steps, and would have a hard time making a terrarium.

English Language Arts 30

Spectrum Test Prep Grade 3

30

Use Tools to Find Information
Reading: Informational Text

DIRECTIONS: Read the passage. Then, choose or write the best answer.

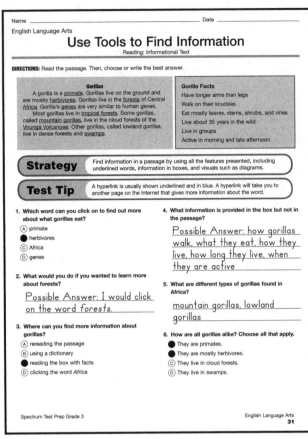

Gorillas

A gorilla is a primate. Gorillas live on the ground and are mostly herbivores. Gorillas live in the forests of Central Africa. Gorilla's genes are very similar to human genes. Most gorillas live in tropical forests. Some gorillas, called mountain gorillas, live in the cloud forests of the Virunga Volcanoes. Other gorillas, called lowland gorillas, live in dense forests and swamps.

Gorilla Facts
- Have longer arms than legs
- Walk on their knuckles
- Eat mostly leaves, stems, shrubs, and vines
- Live about 35 years in the wild
- Live in groups
- Active in morning and late afternoon

Strategy Find information in a passage by using all the features presented, including underlined words, information in boxes, and visuals such as diagrams.

Test Tip A hyperlink is usually shown underlined and in blue. A hyperlink will take you to another page on the Internet that gives more information about the word.

1. Which word can you click on to find out more about what gorillas eat?
   - (A) primate
   - ● herbivores
   - (C) Africa
   - (D) genes

2. What would you do if you wanted to learn more about forests?

   Possible Answer: I would click on the word forests.

3. Where can you find more information about gorillas?
   - (A) rereading the passage
   - (B) using a dictionary
   - ● reading the box with facts
   - (D) clicking the word Africa

4. What information is provided in the box but not in the passage?

   Possible Answer: how gorillas walk, what they eat, how they live, how long they live, when they are active

5. What are different types of gorillas found in Africa?

   mountain gorillas, lowland gorillas

6. How are all gorillas alike? Choose all that apply.
   - ● They are primates.
   - ● They are mostly herbivores.
   - (C) They live in cloud forests.
   - (D) They live in swamps.

English Language Arts
31

31

Use Tools to Find Information
Reading: Informational Text

DIRECTIONS: Read the passage. Then, choose or write the best answer.

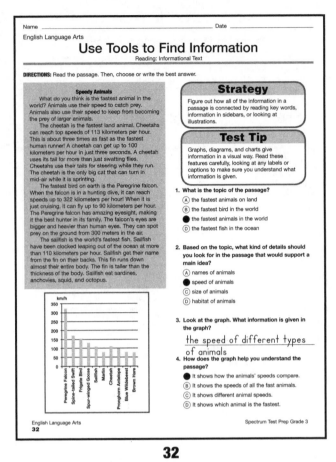

Speedy Animals

What do you think is the fastest animal in the world? Animals use their speed to catch prey. Animals also use their speed to keep from becoming the prey of larger animals.

The cheetah is the fastest land animal. Cheetahs can reach top speeds of 113 kilometers per hour. This is about three times as fast as the fastest human runner! A cheetah can get up to 100 kilometers per hour in just three seconds. A cheetah uses its tail for more than just swatting flies. Cheetahs use their tails for steering while they run. The cheetah is the only big cat that can turn in mid-air while it is sprinting.

The fastest bird on earth is the Peregrine falcon. When the falcon is in a hunting dive, it can reach speeds up to 322 kilometers per hour. When it is just cruising, it can fly up to 90 kilometers per hour. The Peregrine falcon has amazing eyesight, making it the best hunter in its family. The falcon's eyes are bigger and heavier than human eyes. They can spot prey on the ground from 300 meters in the air.

The sailfish is the world's fastest fish. Sailfish have been clocked leaping out of the ocean at more than 110 kilometers per hour. Sailfish get their name from the fin on their backs. This fin runs down almost their entire body. The fin is taller than the thickness of the body. Sailfish eat sardines, anchovies, squid, and octopus.

Strategy Figure out how all of the information in a passage is connected by reading key words, information in sidebars, or looking at illustrations.

Test Tip Graphs, diagrams, and charts give information in a visual way. Read these features carefully, looking at any labels or captions to make sure you understand what information is given.

1. What is the topic of the passage?
   - (A) the fastest animals on land
   - (B) the fastest bird in the world
   - ● the fastest animals in the world
   - (D) the fastest fish in the ocean

2. Based on the topic, what kind of details should you look for in the passage that would support a main idea?
   - (A) names of animals
   - ● speed of animals
   - (C) size of animals
   - (D) habitat of animals

3. Look at the graph. What information is given in the graph?

   the speed of different types of animals

4. How does the graph help you understand the passage?
   - ● It shows how the animals' speeds compare.
   - (B) It shows the speeds of all the fast animals.
   - (C) It shows different animal speeds.
   - (D) It shows which animal is the fastest.

Spectrum Test Prep Grade 3

32

Identify Point of View
Reading: Informational Text

DIRECTIONS: Choose or write the best answer.

School Uniforms

Students in Kenosha Schools should have to wear uniforms. Students who wear uniforms do better in school. There is less bullying because students are not teased about their clothes. Students can focus on schoolwork instead of on what everyone is wearing. School uniforms also save families money. Parents don't have to buy their children a lot of new school clothes every year. Parents can just buy a few uniforms for their children to wear.

Strategy As you read, look for the author's point of view, or what he or she thinks, feels, or believes about the topic. Compare the author's point of view to your own.

Test Tip Authors write passages to share their ideas and opinions on a topic. The author should include details that support their thoughts or opinions.

1. What is the author's opinion?

   Students in Kenosha Schools should wear uniforms.

2. Write two details that support the opinion you wrote above.

   Possible Answers: Students do better in school. Students focus on schoolwork. Families save money.

3. Which detail does NOT support the author's point of view?
   - (A) Students who wear uniforms do better in school.
   - (B) School uniforms save families money.
   - ● School uniforms are usually boring.
   - (D) School uniforms cut down on bullying.

4. How can school uniforms help students focus on schoolwork?

   Possible Answers: Instead of thinking about what to wear each day, students can spend that time on homework and studying.

5. Why does the author think that school uniforms cut down on bullying?
   - ● Students can't tease each other about their clothes.
   - (B) Students focus on their work and not on what others are wearing.
   - (C) Parents can just buy a few uniforms.
   - (D) Students don't need to buy a lot of new clothes each year.

6. Do you agree or disagree with the author's point of view? Explain.

   Possible Answer: I disagree. I think it is important for students to be able to show their personality through how they dress.

English Language Arts
33

33

Identify Point of View
Reading: Informational Text

DIRECTIONS: Read the passage. Then, choose or write the best answer.

A Winter Day

Ah, a winter's day is a beautiful gift! How I love the feel of light, fluffy snowflakes on my face, the brisk, chill air through my hair, and the bite of the cold on my nose. There is always plenty of play on a cold day, too. To run through the snow is a joy. To slide on the ice, a sweet dance. To fly down the hill on slippery snow and ice is a thrill! Such a day is never a waste. A time to be free, a time to play. Oh, the winter is joy, is happiness. The snow, the cold, the clean air is a special gift!

Strategy Identify the author's point of view by finding words that show feelings or thoughts about how they feel about a topic. Compare your feelings about the topic to the author's feelings.

Test Tip Authors share facts about topics. Sometimes, authors also share what they think or how they feel about a topic.

1. How does the author of the passage feel about winter?
   - (A) hates winter
   - ● loves winter
   - (C) thinks winter is boring
   - (D) wishes winter would end

2. Write words that the author uses to show his or her feelings.

   Possible Answer: snowflakes on his face, running through snow, sledding

3. Why might the author have written this passage?
   - (A) to share ideas about winter activities
   - (B) to give reasons to stay inside in the cold
   - ● to present an opinion about winter
   - (D) to give facts about the seasons

4. If a person who didn't like winter read this passage, how do you think they would feel about it? Explain your answer.

   Possible Answer: If a person who didn't like winter read this poem, they might find it unbelievable that the author likes the cold and snow.

5. Would someone who loves summer like reading this passage? Explain.

   Possible Answer: No. He or she would disagree strongly with the author and not enjoy reading the passage.

6. Do you agree with the author? Explain your answer.

   Possible Answers: Yes. I think it is fun to play outside in the snow. No. Winter is too cold to enjoy being outside.

Spectrum Test Prep Grade 3

34

Compare and Contrast Texts
Reading: Informational Text

DIRECTIONS: Read each passage. Then, choose or write the best answer.

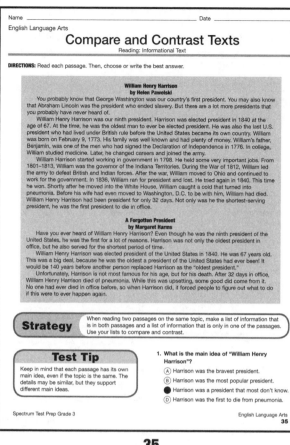

William Henry Harrison
by Helen Pawelski

You probably know that George Washington was our country's first president. You may also know that Abraham Lincoln was the president who ended slavery. But there are a lot more presidents that you probably have never heard of.

William Henry Harrison was our ninth president. Harrison was elected president in 1840 at the age of 67. At the time, he was the oldest man to ever be elected president. He was also the last U.S. president who had lived under British rule before the United States became its own country. William was born on February 9, 1773. His family was well known and had plenty of money. William's father, Benjamin, was one of the men who had signed the Declaration of Independence in 1776. In college, William studied medicine. Later, he changed careers and joined the army.

William Harrison started working in government in 1798. He held some very important jobs. From 1801–1813, William was the governor of the Indiana Territories. During the War of 1812, William led the army to defeat British and Indian forces. After the war, William moved to Ohio and continued to work for the government. In 1836, William ran for president and lost. He tried again in 1840. This time he won. Shortly after he moved into the White House, William caught a cold that turned into pneumonia. Before his wife had even come to Washington, D.C. to be with him, William had died. William Henry Harrison had been president for only 32 days. Not only was he the shortest-serving president, he was the first president to die in office.

A Forgotten President
by Margaret Harms

Have you ever heard of William Henry Harrison? Even though he was the ninth president of the United States, he was the first for a lot of reasons. Harrison was not only the oldest president in office, but he also served for the shortest period of time.

William Henry Harrison was elected president of the United States in 1840. He was 67 years old. This was a big deal, because he was the oldest a president of the United States had ever been! It would be 140 years before another person replaced Harrison as the "oldest president."

Unfortunately, Harrison is not most famous for his age, but for his death. After 32 days in office, William Henry Harrison died of pneumonia. While this was upsetting, some good did come from it. No one had ever died in office before, so when Harrison did, it forced people to figure out what to do if this were to ever happen again.

Strategy When reading two passages on the same topic, make a list of information that is in both passages and a list of information that is only in one of the passages. Use your lists to compare and contrast.

Test Tip Keep in mind that each passage has its own main idea, even if the topic is the same. The details may be similar, but they support different main ideas.

1. What is the main idea of "William Henry Harrison"?
   (A) Harrison was the bravest president.
   (B) Harrison was the most popular president.
   ● Harrison was a president that most don't know.
   (D) Harrison was the first to die from pneumonia.

35

Compare and Contrast Texts
Reading: Informational Texts

DIRECTIONS: Choose or write the best answer.

Strategy Identify the main idea of each passage by using the facts, ideas, or opinions that the authors share in each passage.

Test Tip Different passages on the same topic will have details that are unique, or details that one passage has that the other does not have.

2. What is the main idea of "A Forgotten President"?
   (A) Harrison was should not have been president.
   ● Harrison had a lot of firsts in his presidency.
   (C) Harrison set a record that was never broken.
   (D) Harrison was seriously ill but still elected.

3. Compare the two passages. What do these two passages have in common?

   Both share details about Harrison's presidency.

4. Reread each passage. What information is given in the first passage that is not included in the second passage?

   information about Harrison's life

5. Use details from the first passage to put the events that led to Harrison's presidency in order. Write the numbers 2, 3, 4, and 5.
   [1] Harrison went to medical school.
   [5] Harrison lost the election in 1836.
   [3] Harrison was the governor for the Indiana territories.
   [2] Harrison joined the army.
   [4] Harrison led the army to defeat British and Indian forces.

6. What information is given in the second passage that is not included in the first passage?

   a detail about how Harrison's death forced leaders to figure out what to do if a president dies

7. Why does the author of the second passage call Harrison's death "good"?

   It made people figure out what to do if another president died in office.

Write the key detail that helped you answer the question above.

   "No one had ever died in office before, so when Harrison did, it forced people to figure out what to do if this were to ever happen again."

36

Compare and Contrast Texts
Reading: Informational Texts

DIRECTIONS: Use the passages to choose or write the best answer.

Strategy As you read two passages on the same topic, determine how the main idea of each passage is similar and different. Use the most important ideas and details to identify the main idea of each passage.

Test Tip Comparing and contrasting is easier to do if you organize your ideas. Make a chart to list details that are the same and details that are different.

1. What is the main idea of both passages?
   (A) Butterflies and moths are different insects.
   ● Butterflies and moths are similar in many ways.
   (C) Butterflies and moths both start their lives as caterpillars.
   (D) Butterflies are prettier than moths.

2. Why do some butterflies and moths have brightly colored wings?

   The colors warn predators that the butterflies are poisonous.

3. Reread each passage. Write one key detail from each passage about how butterflies and moths protect themselves.

   Possible Answer: First passage—Caterpillars have color patterns for camouflage. They have bright colors to warn predators that they are deadly. Second passage—To warn predators, these caterpillars are brightly colored. Predators know not to eat them

4. Are the details you wrote for #3 important? How do the details support the main idea?

   Possible Answer: Yes. Details about how butterflies and moths protect each other is important information. Both details support the main idea because they show how butterflies and insects are alike.

5. Write a key detail that tells how moths and butterflies are different from other insects.

   Possible Answer: "Adult moths and butterflies have a special mouth that no other insect has."

6. Write two key details about how moths and butterflies are different.

   Possible Answers: Butterfly antennae have a thick part at the end, but moth antennae are thin all the way to the tip. Butterflies hold their wings up and over their bodies, but moths fold their wings under their bodies.

38

Determine the Meaning of Words and Phrases
Language

DIRECTIONS: Choose or write the best answer.

Strategy To determine the meaning of an unknown word, look at the words and phrases around the unknown word. These are clues to the meaning.

Test Tip Think about the meaning of the sentence as a whole. Then, choose the meaning that fits with the sentence.

1. Anna used the garden _____ to wash the dog.
   (A) rake
   (B) seeds
   ● hose
   (D) gate

   All of these words are objects used in a garden. Write how you chose the correct answer.

   Possible Answer: I used the context of washing the dog to realize that Anna would need water from a hose.

2. The thrilling ride on the roller coaster made us yell loudly.
   Choose two words that mean the same as thrilling.
   ● exciting
   (B) boring
   (C) slow
   ● awesome

3. Write a word to complete this sentence.
   The _____ weather will continue all night, but we will be safe and sound inside.

   Possible Answers: stormy, rainy, scary, snowy, windy
   What context clues helped you write your answer?

   Possible Answers: weather; safe and sound inside

4. Before Samantha awoke, I left her present beside her bed.
   What does the word awoke mean?

   woke up

   How did looking at the parts of the word awoke help you determine its meaning?
   Possible Answer: I knew the root word was woke and I have seen the word awake before. If you are awake, you are not sleeping anymore.

5. Sam's grades have really improved. He had a C at the beginning of the year, and now he has an A.
   What does improved mean?
   ● gotten better
   (B) gotten worse
   (C) fixed
   (D) dropped

6. Sarah is being very disagreeable today.
   What does the word disagreeable mean?

   Possible Answer: She won't agree to anything. She is unhappy.

39

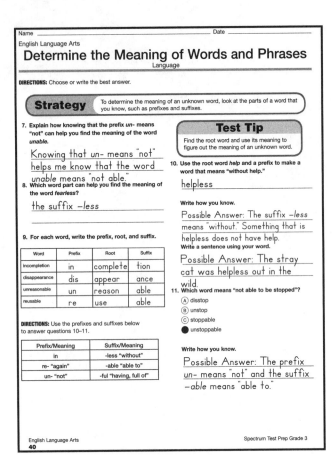

English Language Arts
Determine the Meaning of Words and Phrases
Language

DIRECTIONS: Choose or write the best answer.

Strategy To determine the meaning of an unknown word, look at the parts of a word that you know, such as prefixes and suffixes.

7. Explain how knowing that the prefix *un-* means "not" can help you find the meaning of the word *unable*.

Knowing that un- means "not" helps me know that the word *unable* means "not able."

8. Which word part can help you find the meaning of the word *fearless*?

the suffix *–less*

9. For each word, write the prefix, root, and suffix.

Word	Prefix	Root	Suffix
incompletion	in	complete	tion
disappearance	dis	appear	ance
unreasonable	un	reason	able
reusable	re	use	able

DIRECTIONS: Use the prefixes and suffixes below to answer questions 10–11.

Prefix/Meaning	Suffix/Meaning
in	-less "without"
re- "again"	-able "able to"
un- "not"	-ful "having, full of"

Test Tip Find the root word and use its meaning to figure out the meaning of an unknown word.

10. Use the root word *help* and a prefix to make a word that means "without help."

helpless

Write how you know.

Possible Answer: The suffix *–less* means "without." Something that is helpless does not have help.

Write a sentence using your word.

Possible Answer: The stray cat was helpless out in the wild.

11. Which word means "not able to be stopped"?
(A) disstop
(B) unstop
(C) stoppable
● unstoppable

Write how you know.

Possible Answer: The prefix *un-* means "not" and the suffix *–able* means "able to."

English Language Arts
40

Spectrum Test Prep Grade 3

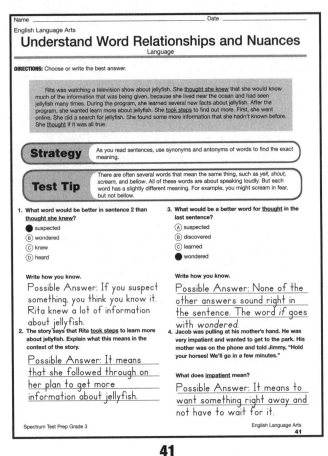

English Language Arts
Understand Word Relationships and Nuances
Language

DIRECTIONS: Choose or write the best answer.

Rita was watching a television show about jellyfish. She thought she knew that she would know much of the information that was being given, because she lived near the ocean and had seen jellyfish many times. During the program, she learned several new facts about jellyfish. After the program, she wanted learn more about jellyfish. She took steps to find out more. First, she went online. She did a search for jellyfish. She found some more information that she hadn't known before. She thought if it was all true.

Strategy As you read sentences, use synonyms and antonyms of words to find the exact meaning.

Test Tip There are often several words that mean the same thing, such as *yell, shout, scream,* and *bellow.* All of these words are about speaking loudly. But each word has a slightly different meaning. For example, you might scream in fear, but not bellow.

1. What word would be better in sentence 2 than thought she knew?
● suspected
(B) wondered
(C) knew
(D) heard

Write how you know.

Possible Answer: If you suspect something, you think you know it. Rita knew a lot of information about jellyfish.

2. The story says that Rita took steps to learn more about jellyfish. Explain what this means in the context of the story.

Possible Answer: It means that she followed through on her plan to get more information about jellyfish.

3. What would be a better word for thought in the last sentence?
(A) suspected
(B) discovered
(C) learned
● wondered

Write how you know.

Possible Answer: None of the other answers sound right in the sentence. The word *if* goes with *wondered.*

4. Jacob was pulling at his mother's hand. He was very impatient and wanted to get to the park. His mother was on the phone and told Jimmy, "Hold your horses! We'll go in a few minutes."

What does impatient mean?

Possible Answer: It means to want something right away and not have to wait for it.

Spectrum Test Prep Grade 3

English Language Arts
41

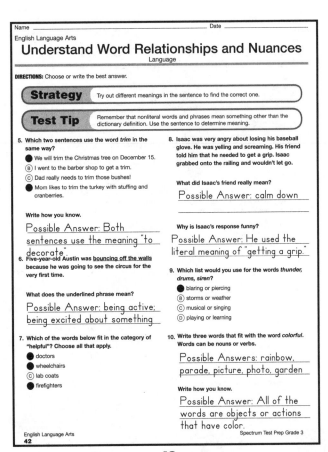

English Language Arts
Understand Word Relationships and Nuances
Language

DIRECTIONS: Choose or write the best answer.

Strategy Try out different meanings in the sentence to find the correct one.

Test Tip Remember that nonliteral words and phrases mean something other than the dictionary definition. Use the sentence to determine meaning.

5. Which two sentences use the word *trim* in the same way?
● We will trim the Christmas tree on December 15.
(B) I went to the barber shop to get a trim.
(C) Dad really needs to trim those bushes!
● Mom likes to trim the turkey with stuffing and cranberries.

Write how you know.

Possible Answer: Both sentences use the meaning "to decorate."

6. Five-year-old Austin was bouncing off the walls because he was going to see the circus for the very first time.

What does the underlined phrase mean?

Possible Answer: being active; being excited about something

7. Which of the words below fit in the category of "helpful"? Choose all that apply.
● doctors
● wheelchairs
(C) lab coats
● firefighters

8. Isaac was very angry about losing his baseball glove. He was yelling and screaming. His friend told him that he needed to get a grip. Isaac grabbed onto the railing and wouldn't let go.

What did Isaac's friend really mean?

Possible Answer: calm down

Why is Isaac's response funny?

Possible Answer: He used the literal meaning of "getting a grip."

9. Which list would you use for the words *thunder, drums, siren*?
● blaring or piercing
(B) storms or weather
(C) musical or singing
(D) playing or learning

10. Write three words that fit with the word *colorful.* Words can be nouns or verbs.

Possible Answers: rainbow, parade, picture, photo, garden

Write how you know.

Possible Answer: All of the words are objects or actions that have color.

English Language Arts
42

Spectrum Test Prep Grade 3

English Language Arts
Write an Opinion
Writing

DIRECTIONS: An opinion paragraph tells what you think or how you feel about a topic. It gives reasons why you think or feel that way. Write an opinion paragraph for the school newspaper about a book that everyone in your class should read. Your paragraph should have:
- A sentence to introduce your topic
- A statement of your opinion
- An organizational structure
- Reasons to support your opinion
- Linking words and phrases to connect your opinion and reasons
- A sentence to end your paragraph

Strategy Plan your writing by stating your opinion and listing reasons you have that opinion. Then, begin writing. When you are finished writing, read your paragraph to yourself. Make sure you included everything listed in the directions. Make sure your writing is clear and fix any errors.

Test Tip An opinion must be supported with reasons. Reasons tell why you think or feel a certain way. Include details from the book that support your reasons.

Everyone should read the book:	
Reason 1:	
Details:	Answers will vary.
Reason 2:	
Details:	
Reason 3:	
Details:	
Conclusion:	

Spectrum Test Prep Grade 3

English Language Arts
43

English Language Arts

Write an Opinion
Writing

DIRECTIONS: Write your paragraph on the lines Use the checklist to make sure your paragraph has all of the parts needed.

Test Tip Use your graphic organizer as you write to keep your ideas organized and so you don't forget to include an idea or detail.

Checklist
- ☐ I introduced my topic.
- ☐ I stated my opinion.
- ☐ I gave at least two reasons for my opinion.
- ☐ I supported my reasons with details.
- ☐ I used linking words.
- ☐ I have a good conclusion.
- ☐ My sentences all make sense.
- ☐ I used nouns and verbs correctly.
- ☐ I used capital letters properly.
- ☐ I used correct punctuation.
- ☐ I spelled all of my words correctly.

Student should:
- introduce the topic
- state an opinion
- supply several reasons for the opinion
- include details to support reasons
- provide a sense of closure
- use linking words

44

English Language Arts

Write an Informative Text
Writing

DIRECTIONS: An informative text gives facts and details about a topic. Write an informative text about a pet or an animal that you know a lot about. Your paragraph should have:

- A sentence to introduce your topic
- Facts about your subject
- Definitions and details about your subject
- Linking words and phrases to connect your ideas
- A sentence to end your paragraph

Strategy Plan your writing by listing details that relate to your topic or facts. Then, begin writing. When you are finished writing, read your paragraph to yourself. Make sure you included everything listed in the directions. Make sure your writing is clear and fix any errors.

Test Tip Facts are information that is true. Informative pieces can give opinions, but they mostly give facts about a topic. Try to think of at least two details for each fact.

Topic:	
Fact 1:	Answer:
Details:	Paragraphs will vary.
Fact 2:	
Details:	
Fact 3:	
Details:	
Conclusion:	

45

English Language Arts

Write an Informative Text
Writing

DIRECTIONS: Write your paragraph on the lines. Use the checklist to make sure your paragraph has the information needed.

Test Tip Use the graphic organizer with your facts and details to write your informational text. Be sure to connect ideas with linking words.

Checklist
- ☐ I introduced my topic.
- ☐ I gave at least two facts about my topic.
- ☐ I supported my facts with details.
- ☐ I used linking words.
- ☐ I have a good conclusion.
- ☐ My sentences all make sense.
- ☐ I used nouns and verbs correctly.
- ☐ I used capital letters properly.
- ☐ I used correct punctuation.
- ☐ I spelled all of my words correctly.

Student should:
- introduce the topic
- state facts about the topic
- supply several details to support the facts
- provide a sense of closure
- use linking words

46

English Language Arts

Write a Narrative
Writing

DIRECTIONS: A narrative is a story that tells about real or imagined events. Write a narrative about a fun experience you have had. Your paragraph should have:

- A narrator and/or characters
- A natural sequence of events
- Dialogue
- Descriptions of actions, thoughts, and feelings
- Time words and phrases to show the order of events
- A sentence to end your paragraph

Strategy Plan a narrative by choosing people, places, and events that will be in the story. Remember that a story should have a beginning, middle, and end.

Test Tip Include details that help your readers understand the event and imagine it in their minds.

Experience:	
Event 1:	Answer:
Details:	Paragraphs will vary.
Event 2:	
Details:	
Event 3:	
Details:	
Conclusion:	

47

Write a Narrative
Writing

DIRECTIONS: Write your paragraph on the lines. Use the checklist to make sure your paragraph has everything.

Test Tip Use your organizer as you write your narrative to make sure events are in order and that you use details.

Checklist
- ☐ I introduced my narrator and/or characters.
- ☐ I explained the problem in the story.
- ☐ I wrote a clear sequence of events that happened.
- ☐ I used dialogue and wrote about the characters' actions, thoughts, and feelings.
- ☐ I used time words.
- ☐ I have a good conclusion.
- ☐ My sentences all make sense.
- ☐ I used nouns and verbs correctly.
- ☐ I used capital letters properly.
- ☐ I used correct punctuation.
- ☐ I spelled all of my words correctly.

Student should:
- include a narrator and/or characters
- follow a natural sequence of events
- include dialogue
- include descriptions of characters' actions, thoughts, and feelings
- use time words and phrases to show the order of events
- write a satisfying conclusion

48

Understand Editing and Revising
Writing

DIRECTIONS: Read the paragraph. Underline places in the paragraph that are not clear. Then, rewrite the paragraph on the lines so it makes sense.

Strategy Revise to make sure your writing makes sense. Then, edit to fix errors. Use what you know about nouns, verbs, adjectives, and adverbs to make correct choices when you edit.

Test Tip When you are revising a paragraph, read it out loud to yourself. Listen for anything that does not sound right or does not make sense.

Last summer, I went on vacation with my family. We drove across the country. First, we stopped in Sioux Falls. It is in South Dakota. It is very pretty there. We saw the waterfall. The city is named after it. It was very cool. Then, we left and went somewhere else. It was farther west. It was called the Badlands. It is called that because the land is very dry and things can't grow well. We went on a helicopter ride. It was so cool! After South Dakota, we went to Wyoming to see Devil's Tower because my dad really likes *Close Encounters of the Third Kind* and that is where it was made and we went to Colorado. We went rafting and my brother jumped off a big rock. The water was really cold. It was fun when we took the train to the top of Pike's Peak. Then, we drove home. It was a long vacation. It was two weeks. We had a lot of fun.

Possible Answer: Last summer, I went on vacation with my family. We drove across the country for two weeks. First, we stopped in Sioux Falls, South Dakota. It is very pretty there. We saw the waterfall that the city is named after. It was very cool to see a waterfall up close. Next, we went farther west to an area called the Badlands. It is called Badlands because the land is very dry and plants can't grow very well. In the Badlands, we went on a helicopter ride. It was so cool! After South Dakota, we went to Wyoming to see Devil's Tower. Devil's Tower is where the movie Close Encounters of the Third Kind was made. My dad loves that movie! From Wyoming, we drove to Colorado. We went rafting and my brother jumped off a big rock into the river. The water was really cold. We also took a train to the top of Pike's Peak. Finally, we drove home. We had a lot of fun on our vacation.

49

Understand Editing and Revising
Writing

DIRECTIONS: Read the paragraph. Look for spelling, capitalization, and punctuation mistakes. Rewrite the paragraph correctly on the lines.

Strategy Reread your writing out loud to find punctuation mistakes. To find spelling and capitalization errors, try reading backward, looking at each word.

Last week my family went to an amusement park for the day we went on a lot of rides. My favrit ride was a roller coaster call the demon. The demon goes upside down for times. I was scared at first but my mom went with me and she had gone on it many times since she was my age. Wen we were done on the demon we went on the bumper cars the swings and the log ride. I like to go to the amusement park on wednesday becuz there are not a lot of people and the lines are shortest. Next time we go to the amusement park I want to go on another roller coaster. They are so much fun!

Last week, my family went to an amusement park for the day. We went on a lot of rides. My favorite ride was a roller coaster called the Demon. The Demon goes upside down four times. I was scared at first, but my mom went with me. She had gone on it many times since she was my age. When we were done on the Demon, we went on the bumper cars, the swings, and the log ride. I like to go to the amusement park on Wednesday, because there are not a lot of people and the lines are shorter. Next time we go to the amusement park, I want to go on another roller coaster. They are so much fun!

50

Strategy Review

In this section, you will review the strategies you learned and apply them to practice the skills.

Strategy Use details from a story or passage to show your understanding.

When you read a story, think about how a character's thoughts, words, and actions show how he or she is feeling.

EXAMPLE
Read the story carefully. Then, answer the questions using details from the story.

Juan looked at the clock. He paced across the floor. His best friend, Bill, was coming to visit for the first time in six months. Bill had moved very far away. Juan wondered if they would still feel like good friends.

The doorbell rang, and Juan raced to answer it. Bill looked a bit unsure. Juan smiled and started talking just as he always had when they had lived near one another. He made Bill feel comfortable. As the day went on, it felt like old times.

How do Juan's actions show that he was nervous and excited? Think about how someone might act if he were nervous or excited. Look back at how the author describes Juan's actions. "Juan looked at the clock. He paced across the floor." This is something a person who is excited or nervous would do.

1. Why was Juan so excited about his friend coming over?

His friend had moved far away and they had not seen each other for a long time.

2. How did Juan try to make Bill feel comfortable?

He smiled and started talking just like he always had.

How did the strategy help you answer these questions?

Possible Answer: When I thought about Juan's actions, I was able to understand how he was feeling

Strategy Make a picture in your mind as you read.

Read the story. Then, answer the questions.

One day in the times when the sky was close to the ground, a woman went out to pound rice. Before she began her work, she took off the beads from around her neck and the comb from her hair. She hung the comb and beads in the sky. Then, she began working. Each time she raised her pestle into the air to pound the rice, it hit the sky. The sky began to rise. It went up so far that the woman lost her beads and comb. Never did they come back down, for the comb became the moon and the beads became the stars that are scattered about.

As you read this story, picture a woman kneeling in the sand, with a bowl in front of her. Imagine her take the beads from around her neck and the comb out of her hair and hang them above her head.

3. What else do you see in your mind when you read this story?

Possible Answer: I see the woman pounding the rice in the bowl. I see the beads and comb rising into the sky and turning into the moon and stars.

4. Based on the story, what do you think a *pestle* is?
- ⬤ A a tool for mashing food
- Ⓑ a trinket for holding hair away from the face
- Ⓒ a bowl for holding rice
- Ⓓ a piece of jewelry

Which words helped you determine the meaning?

Possible Answer: pound, raised, rice

51

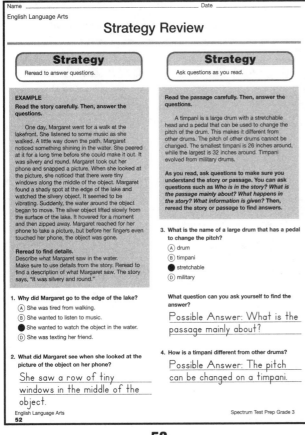

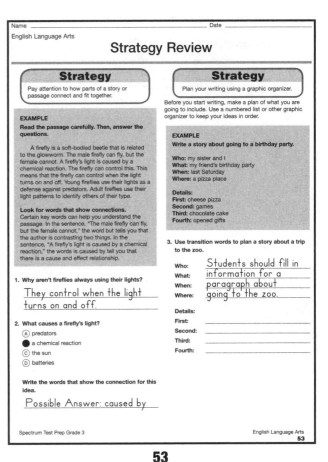

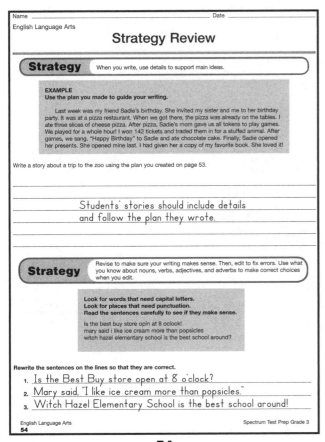

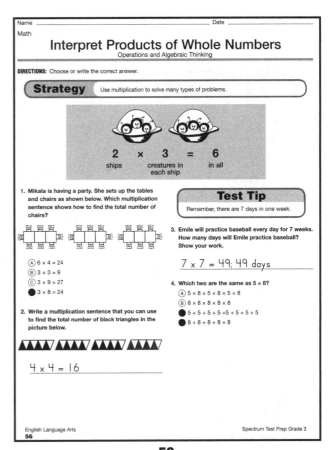

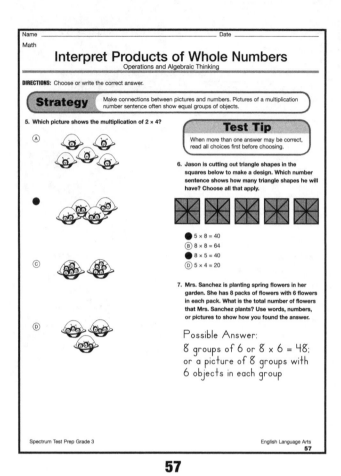

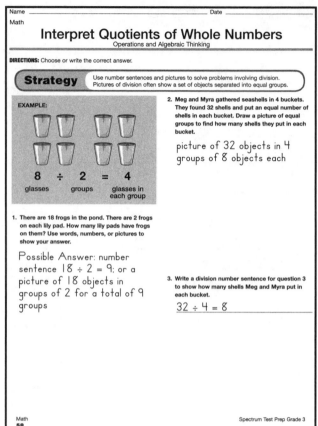

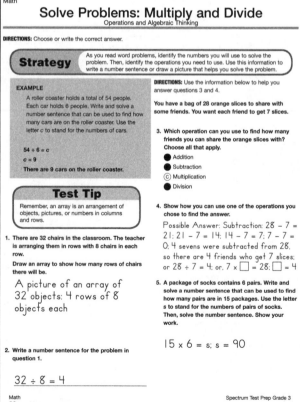

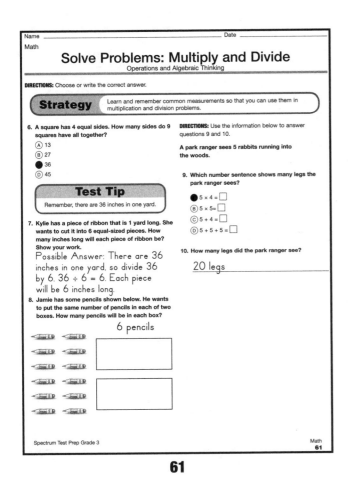

Solve Problems: Multiply and Divide
Operations and Algebraic Thinking

DIRECTIONS: Choose or write the correct answer.

Strategy — Learn and remember common measurements so that you can use them in multiplication and division problems.

6. A square has 4 equal sides. How many sides do 9 squares have all together?
   - Ⓐ 13
   - Ⓑ 27
   - ● 36
   - Ⓓ 45

Test Tip
Remember, there are 36 inches in one yard.

7. Kylie has a piece of ribbon that is 1 yard long. She wants to cut it into 6 equal-sized pieces. How many inches long will each piece of ribbon be? Show your work.

Possible Answer: There are 36 inches in one yard, so divide 36 by 6. 36 ÷ 6 = 6. Each piece will be 6 inches long.

8. Jamie has some pencils shown below. He wants to put the same number of pencils in each of two boxes. How many pencils will be in each box?

6 pencils

DIRECTIONS: Use the information below to answer questions 9 and 10.

A park ranger sees 5 rabbits running into the woods.

9. Which number sentence shows many legs the park ranger sees?
   - ● 5 × 4 = ☐
   - Ⓑ 5 × 5 = ☐
   - Ⓒ 5 + 4 = ☐
   - Ⓓ 5 + 5 + 5 = ☐

10. How many legs did the park ranger see?

20 legs

61

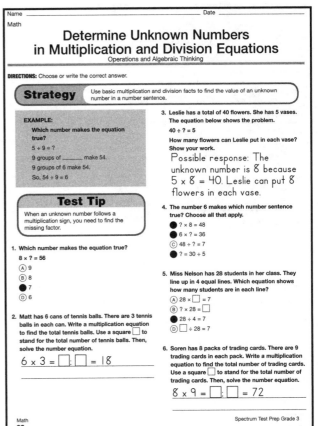

Determine Unknown Numbers in Multiplication and Division Equations
Operations and Algebraic Thinking

DIRECTIONS: Choose or write the correct answer.

Strategy — Use basic multiplication and division facts to find the value of an unknown number in a number sentence.

EXAMPLE:
Which number makes the equation true?
$5 \div 9 = ?$
9 groups of _____ make 54.
9 groups of 6 make 54.
So, $54 \div 9 = 6$

Test Tip
When an unknown number follows a multiplication sign, you need to find the missing factor.

1. Which number makes the equation true?
   $8 \times ? = 56$
   - Ⓐ 9
   - Ⓑ 8
   - ● 7
   - Ⓓ 6

2. Matt has 6 cans of tennis balls. There are 3 tennis balls in each can. Write a multiplication equation to find the total tennis balls. Use a square ☐ to stand for the total number of tennis balls. Then, solve the number equation.

   $6 \times 3 = \boxed{\ }; \boxed{\ } = 18$

3. Leslie has a total of 40 flowers. She has 5 vases. The equation below shows the problem.
   $40 \div ? = 5$
   How many flowers can Leslie put in each vase? Show your work.

   Possible response: The unknown number is 8 because 5 × 8 = 40. Leslie can put 8 flowers in each vase.

4. The number 6 makes which number sentence true? Choose all that apply.
   - ● ? × 8 = 48
   - ● 6 × ? = 36
   - Ⓒ 48 ÷ ? = 7
   - ● ? = 30 ÷ 5

5. Miss Nelson has 28 students in her class. They line up in 4 equal lines. Which equation shows how many students are in each line?
   - Ⓐ 28 × ☐ = 7
   - Ⓑ ? × 28 = 7
   - ● 28 ÷ 4 = 7
   - Ⓓ ☐ ÷ 28 = 7

6. Soren has 8 packs of trading cards. There are 9 trading cards in each pack. Write a multiplication equation to find the total number of trading cards. Use a square ☐ to stand for the total number of trading cards. Then, solve the number equation.

   $8 \times 9 = \boxed{\ }; \boxed{\ } = 72$

62

Determine Unknown Numbers in Multiplication and Division Equations
Operations and Algebraic Thinking

DIRECTIONS: Choose or write the correct answer.

Strategy — To determine the unknown number in a division number sentence, think of a related multiplication fact.

7. Luis has 9 packs of pencils. Each pack contains 5 pencils. Write a number sentence to find how many pencils he has all together.

   $9 \times 5 = 45; 5 \times 9 = 45$

8. Write a word problem that can be solved using the equation below. Then, solve it. Show your work.
   $72 \div 8 = \square$

   Possible Answer: Carlos has a 72-inch long piece of wood to use to make bird houses. He needs 8 inches of wood for the front of each bird house. How many 8-inch long pieces of wood can Carlos cut from his board? Carlos can cut 9 pieces from his board.

9. Ava played in three basketball games. In each of the first two games, she scored 9 points. In the third game, she scored 3 times as many points as in her first two games. Write and solve a number sentence to find how many points she scored in game 3.

   $3 \times 9 = 27$

10. Tamara helps her dad put in a new kitchen floor. She carries 4 boxes of tiles into the kitchen. Each box holds 12 tiles. Which number sentence can be used to show the total number of tiles Tamara carries into the kitchen? Choose all that apply.
    - ● ☐ = 4 × 12
    - Ⓑ 12 − 4 = ☐
    - Ⓒ 48 ÷ 4 = 12
    - ● ☐ ÷ 4 = 12

11. Charlie arranged his book collection of 80 books on 4 shelves. He placed an equal number of books on each shelf. Write and solve a number sentence to find how many books were on each shelf.

    $80 \div 4 = 20$; He placed 20 books on each shelf.

63

Apply Properties of Operations to Multiply and Divide
Operations and Algebraic Thinking

DIRECTIONS: Choose or write the correct answer.

Strategy — Apply multiplication properties to find products. Multiply numbers in any order and any grouping. Use the rules for what happens when a number is multiplied by 0 or 1.

EXAMPLE
The order of numbers does not matter when you multiply.
$6 \times 5 = 5 \times 6$
$30 = 30$

The product stays the same when you change the grouping of the numbers.
$(2 \times 5) \times 6 = 2 \times (5 \times 6)$
$10 \times 6 = 2 \times 30$
$60 = 60$

DIRECTIONS: Write *true* or *false* for questions 1–4.

1. $4 \times 8 = 8 \times 4$ — True
2. $7 \times (4 \times 3) = (7 \times 4) \times 3$ — True
3. $9 \times 8 = 9 \times 9$ — False
4. $(2 \times 6) \times 1 = (1 \times 6) \times 2$ — True

5. Without multiplying, Alvina says that 3 × 4 × 2 has the same product as 2 × 4 × 3. Is Alvina correct? Show your work.

   Possible Answer: Yes, Alvina is correct. The numbers are the same, so their order when multiplying does not matter.

Test Tip
Remember the relationship between multiplication and division. One operation can undo the other.

6. Which two number sentences are BOTH correct?
   - Ⓐ 6 ÷ 1 = 6 and 1 ÷ 6 = 6
   - ● 6 × 1 = 6 and 6 ÷ 6 = 1
   - Ⓒ 6 ÷ 1 = 6 and 6 ÷ 6 = 6
   - Ⓓ 6 × 6 = 6 and 6 ÷ 1 = 6

7. Max says he can multiply the number 114,567 by 0 and get the answer immediately. How can he do that?

   When you multiply any number by 0, the product is always 0. So, 114,567 × 0 = 0.

DIRECTIONS: Use the information that follows to answer questions 8 and 9.

8. Mr. Thompson buys some cases of apples for his store. Each case of apples holds 4 bags of apples. Each bag holds 8 apples. Mr. Thompson buys 2 cases of apples. Which number sentence shows how many apples Mr. Thompson buys? Choose all that apply.
   - ● 2 × 4 × 8 = ☐
   - ● 8 × 8 = ☐
   - Ⓒ 2 × 12 = ☐
   - ● 4 × 8 × 2 = ☐

9. How many apples did Mr. Thompson buy?

   64 apples

64

Apply Properties of Operations to Multiply and Divide
Operations and Algebraic Thinking

DIRECTIONS: Choose or write the correct answer.

Strategy Use your understanding of arrays to solve problems. Sketch an array to show a multiplication problem visually and use the sketch to solve the problem.

10. Dora says there are two correct ways to solve the number sentence below. The two ways are shown. Is Dora correct? Show why or why not.

$12 \div 4 \times 3 = ?$

One Way	Another Way
$(12 \div 4) \times 3$	$12 \div (4 \times 3)$

Possible Answer: No, Dora is not correct. The answers are different. When using all multiplication, the order does not matter. But it does matter when division is used. The order to solve would be parentheses, then multiplication, and then division. So, $(12 \div 4) \times 3 = 3 \times 3 = 9$; and $12 \div (4 \times 3) = 12 \div 12 = 1$

11. Which is NOT a correct way to solve $2 \times 4 \times 3$?
● First, multiply 2×4, then multiply 2×3, finally add the products.
Ⓑ First, multiply 2×4, then multiply 8×3.
Ⓒ First, multiply 2×3, then multiply 6×4.
Ⓓ First, multiply 4×3, then multiply 12×2.

Test Tip
Remember, a 6-by-7 array is the same as a 7-by-6 array.

12. Dimitri has 7 action figures displayed on 6 shelves in his room. Hui has 6 action figures displayed on 7 shelves. Who has more action figures on their shelves? Show your work. Use words, numbers, or pictures.

Possible Answer: They both have the same number of action figures. With numbers: $6 \times 7 = 7 \times 6$. They each have 42 figures. With picture: show 6 rows with 7 objects on each row and 7 rows with 6 objects in each row; the total is the same, 42.

13. Which is the same as 9×6? Choose all that apply.
● $9 \times (4 + 2)$
● $9 \times (3 + 3)$
● $(9 \times 4) + (9 \times 2)$
Ⓓ $3 \times 3 + (4 \times 2)$

65

Understand Division as an Unknown Factor Problem
Operations and Algebraic Thinking

Strategy Solve division problems by representing them as unknown factor multiplication problems.

EXAMPLE
Multiplication and division are inverse operations.
$3 \times 9 = 27$ $9 \times 3 = 27$
$27 \div 9 = 3$ $27 \div 3 = 9$

DIRECTIONS: Use the following information to answer questions 1 and 2.

24 students are divided into groups for a playground game. There are 8 students in each group.

1. June knows that $3 \times 8 = 24$. How can she use that fact to find how many groups there are?

Possible Answer: Multiplication and division are inverse operations. June can divide 24 by 8 to find the number of groups.

2. Write a division equation to solve the problem. Show your work.

Possible Answer: There are 3 groups: $24 \div 8 = 3$

3. Tran has 27 apples. He puts 9 apples in each box. Tran wrote the division sentence below to show how many boxes of apples he has. Which number sentence can be used to find the number of boxes?

$27 \div 9 = \square$

● $9 \times \square = 27$
Ⓑ $27 - 3 = \square$
Ⓒ $9 \times 27 = \square$
Ⓓ $\square \div 9 = 27$

Test Tip
Use what you know about fact families to write related multiplication and division facts.

4. $64 \div 8 = \square$
$8 \times \square = 64$
Ⓐ $\square = 64$
Ⓑ $\square = 56$
Ⓒ $\square = 16$
● $\square = 8$

5. Which can be used to find the answer to 30 divided by 5? Choose all that apply.
Ⓐ $35 - 5 = 30$
● $6 \times 5 = 30$
Ⓒ $5 + 25 = 30$
● $5 \times 6 = 30$

66

Understand Division as an Unknown Factor Problem
Operations and Algebraic Thinking

Strategy Use division as an unknown factor problem. Find the quotient and one factor to find the unknown factor.

6. Explain how to find the number that makes this number sentence true.

$36 \div \square = 9$

Possible Answer: Find the number that makes 36 when multiplied by 9; the number is 4.

7. Which operation sign belongs in each box? Write $+$, $-$, $\times$ or $\div$ in the box.

$42 \boxed{\div} 7 = 6$ $6 \boxed{\times} 7 = 42$

$7 \boxed{\times} 6 = 42$ $42 \boxed{\div} 6 = 7$

DIRECTIONS: Use this information to answer questions 8 and 9.

Benita has a bag of 18 fruit slices to share with her 6 friends.

8. Write a division number sentence to find how many slices each friend will get.

$18 \div 6 = 3$

9. Write two multiplication sentences you can use to check your work.

$3 \times 6 = 18, 6 \times 3 = 18$

10. Leo puts together model cars. He has 13 cars and each car has 3 stickers. Leo wrote the number sentence below to show how many stickers in all are on his 13 cars.

$13 \times 3 = \square$

Write a division number sentence that shows how many stickers are on each car.

$39 \div 3 = 13$

67

Use Strategies to Multiply and Divide Within 100
Operations and Algebraic Thinking

DIRECTIONS: Choose or write the correct answer.

Strategy Use your understanding of related operations to find an unknown number or amount. Rewrite multiplication problems as division problems. Rewrite division problems as multiplication problems.

EXAMPLE
Multiplication and division are related operations.
If you know that $6 \times 4 = 24$, then you know that $24 \div 4 = 6$.

1. A dripping faucet leaks 3 gallons of water a day. If the faucet leaks for 9 days, how many gallons of water does the faucet leak?
Ⓐ 39 gallons
● 27 gallons
Ⓒ 3 gallons
Ⓓ 36 gallons

2. Which of the following does NOT equal 9?
Ⓐ 3×3
Ⓑ $27 \div 3$
● $2 \times 2 \times 3$
Ⓓ $18 \div 2$

3. At the grocery store, apples are arranged in 8 rows with 6 apples in each row. How many apples are there in all? Write how you know.

Possible Answer: 48 apples; I multiply 8 by 6 to get 48.

4. If $7 \times 8 = 56$, then $56 \div \square = 7$
Ⓐ $\square = 5$
Ⓑ $\square = 6$
Ⓒ $\square = 7$
● $\square = 8$

Test Tip
You can check your answers in a division problem by multiplying your answer by the divisor.

5. Mario solved a problem in math class. He checked his answer by using the number sentence $4 \times 7 = \square$. Which problem could Mario have been checking?
● $28 \div 7 = \square$
Ⓑ $42 \div 7 = \square$
Ⓒ $14 \div 7 = \square$
Ⓓ $21 \div 7 = \square$

6. Elli solved $45 \div 9 = \square$ in math class. Her answer was 5. Write a number sentence Elli could use to check her answer. Was she correct?

$5 \times 9 = 45$; She was correct.

68

Use Strategies to Multiply and Divide Within 100
Operations and Algebraic Thinking

DIRECTIONS: Choose or write the correct answer.

Strategy Use multiplication and division to solve different kinds of real-life problems. For example, you use multiplication to find area and to convert feet to inches.

7. What number correctly completes each number sentence?

$63 \div 9 = ?$

$9 \times ? = 63$

_7_

8. Jonas and Emilio are working on an airplane model. Jonas has a piece of wood that is 15 cm long. His piece is 3 times as long as a piece of wood that Emilio has. How long is Emilio's piece of wood? Show your work.

$15 \div 3 = 5$; or $3 \times ? = 15$
Emilio's piece of wood is 5 cm.

Test Tip
To find the area of a rectangle, multiply the length times the width.

9. What is the area of this rectangle? Show your work.

9 feet

8 feet

$9 \times 8 = 72$

_72_ square feet

10. How many inches are in 2 feet? (1 foot = 12 inches)
   Ⓐ 18 inches
   Ⓑ 36 inches
   ● 24 inches
   Ⓓ 12 inches

11. Rhea says that $9 \div 1 = 1$. Her answer is wrong. Find the correct answer and write how you know.

Possible Answer: $9 \div 1 = 9$; any number divided by 1 equals that number.

69

Solve Two-step Problems: Add, Subtract, Multiply, and Divide
Operations and Algebraic Thinking

DIRECTIONS: Choose or write the correct answer.

Strategy When determining how to solve a problem, break it down into steps. Write the operation needed for each step.

EXAMPLE:
Mike's science class is studying 15 kinds of plants. On Monday, they studied 5 plants and on Tuesday they studied 4 plants. How many plants do they still need to study? Write a number sentence and find the answer.
One way to solve this problem is in two steps.
First, you add. Then, you subtract.
Answer: $15 - (5 + 4) = ?$
$15 - 9 = ?$
$? = 6$
There are 6 plants left to be studied.

1. Isabel, Maria, and Lucas decided to weigh their dogs. The weights are shown in the table below. What is the total weight of the three dogs? Write a number sentence and find the answer.

Isabel's Dog	45 pounds
Maria's Dog	32 pounds
Lucas's Dog	56 pounds

133 pounds;
$45 + 32 + 56 = 133$

2. Janna invited 15 girls and 13 boys to her party. She plans to give each of her guests 2 balloons and keep one for herself. How many balloons will Janna need in all?
   Ⓐ 28 balloons
   ● 57 balloons
   Ⓒ 30 balloons
   Ⓓ 29 balloons

3. A music store hopes to have a total of 1,000 customers during the first three months it is open. It had 257 customers the first month and 362 customers the next month. How many customers does the store need during the third month to make its 1,000-customer goal? Show your work.

Possible Answer: 381 customers; add 257 + 362 to get 619; then subtract 619 from 1,000 to get 381

Test Tip
You can check if your answers are reasonable by estimating.

4. Isabella added 36, 19, and 53. She said that the answer was 137. Is this close to the correct answer? Show how rounding can be used to show why or why not.

Possible Answer: No. Isabella's answer is not close because 36 rounds to 40, 19 rounds to 20, and 53 rounds to 50; 40 + 20 + 50 = 110. 110 is not close to 137.

5. A dog sitter works for 4 hours and earns $5 an hour. Then, he works 5 hours and earns $6 an hour. Which number sentence shows how to find the amount of money the dog sitter earns all together?
   Ⓐ $4 \times 6 + 5 \times 5 = \square$
   Ⓑ $4 + 5 + 5 + 6 = \square$
   Ⓒ $20 - 5 \times 6 = \square$
   ● $4 \times 5 + 5 \times 6 = \square$

70

Solve Two-step Problems: Add, Subtract, Multiply, and Divide
Operations and Algebraic Thinking

DIRECTIONS: Choose or write the correct answer.

Strategy Look for clue words in a problem that tell you the operation that is needed. For example, how many means using addition and fewer means subtraction.

6. Chris bakes 3 trays of cookies. Each tray holds 36 cookies. When he takes the cookies out of the oven, he drops 12 cookies. Write and solve a number sentence to find how many cookies Chris has left.

$3 \times 36 - 12 = ?$; $? = 96$; 96 cookies left.

Test Tip
Remember, to find the perimeter of a rectangle, you can add the four sides together or multiply 2 times the length and 2 times the width, and then add.

7. A rectangle has a length of 12 meters and width of 6 meters. Kenji used multiplication and addition to find the perimeter of the rectangle. Show what Kenji's work might look like. Write the answer.

$2 \times 12 + 2 \times 6 = 24 + 12 = 36$; 36 meters

DIRECTIONS: Each package has 5 markers. Use the information that follows to answer questions 8 and 9.

8. Mrs. Chen bought markers. She bought 2 packages of markers for each of the 6 students in her after-school art class. Use the letter m to stand for the total number of markers Mrs. Chen bought and write a number sentence that shows this problem.

$m = 2 \times 6 \times 5$

9. Solve the number sentence to find the total number of markers, m, that Mrs. Chen bought.

$m = 60$ markers

10. Bianca and her family are taking a car trip. On Friday, they drove 279 miles. On Saturday, they drove 508 miles. Bianca estimated that they drove about a total of 800 miles. Is Bianca correct about the total number of miles driven? Use numbers or words to show why or why not.

Possible Answer: Yes, Bianca is correct. You can round 279 to 300 and 508 to 500; 300 + 500 = 800. If you add 279 and 508, you get 787, which is close to 800.

11. A store has 476 DVDs on the shelf. The store receives 2 more cases of DVDs, with 100 DVDs in each. How many DVDs does the store have now?
   Ⓐ 478 DVDs
   Ⓑ 276 DVDs
   ● 676 DVDs
   Ⓓ 576 DVDs

71

Identify and Explain Arithmetic Patterns; Addition and Multiplication
Operations and Algebraic Thinking

DIRECTIONS: Choose or write the correct answer.

Strategy Read patterns closely to know if you need to use addition or multiplication. Make sure to use the numbers already provided in the pattern.

Test Tip Arithmetic patterns are patterns that change by the same rate, such as adding the same number.

EXAMPLE
Find the missing number in the table.

IN	3	8	13	19
OUT	5	10		21

First, look for a pattern in the IN and OUT numbers in the table.
Next, decide what operation you need to use to get from the IN number to the OUT number under it.
Then, to get each OUT number, add 2 to the IN number.
So, the missing number in the table is 13 + 2, which is 15.

DIRECTIONS: Use the addition table to answer questions 1–4.

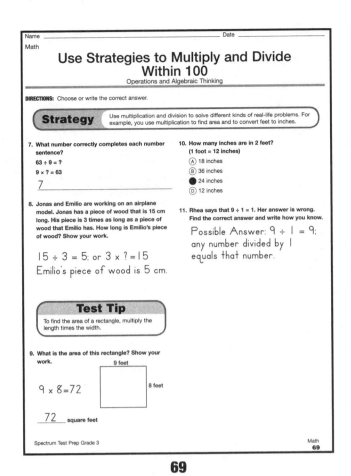

1. What pattern do you see in the sum when you add two EVEN numbers? Write two examples shown in the table.

Possible Answer: The sum of two even numbers is always even. For example, $4 + 6 = 10$ and $6 + 8 = 14$.

2. What pattern do you see in the sum when you add two ODD numbers? Write two examples shown in the table.

Possible Answer: The sum of two odd numbers is always even. For example, $3 + 3 = 6$ and $9 + 5 = 14$.

3. Kyle notices that in each column and each row in the addition table, the even and odd numbers take turns, or alternate. Write why this is. Show an example from the table.

Possible Answer: Each time you move to the right in the table one box or down one box, you add one more to the sum. Adding 1 to an odd number gives an even number, and adding 1 to an even number gives an odd number. For example, in the fourth row, going across, $4 + 1 = 5$, an odd number; then $5 + 1 = 6$, an even number.

4. Look at the diagonal line drawn through the 10s in the table. The line shows the different ways of writing 10 as a sum. Write three number sentences with sums of 10 shown in the table.

Possible Answer: $8 + 2 = 10$, $7 + 3 = 10$, $4 + 6 = 10$

72

Identify and Explain Arithmetic Patterns; Addition and Multiplication
Operations and Algebraic Thinking

DIRECTIONS: Use the multiplication table to answer questions 5–8.

Strategy — When solving a pattern, try writing number sentences that work for the numbers shown.

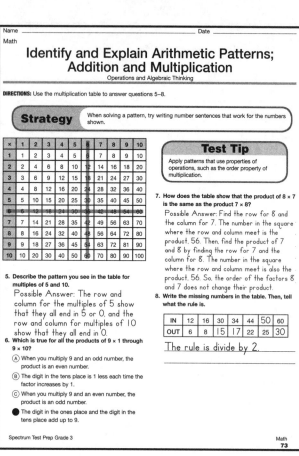

Test Tip

Apply patterns that use properties of operations, such as the order property of multiplication.

×	1	2	3	4	5	6	7	8	9	10
1	1	2	3	4	5	6	7	8	9	10
2	2	4	6	8	10	12	14	16	18	20
3	3	6	9	12	15	18	21	24	27	30
4	4	8	12	16	20	24	28	32	36	40
5	5	10	15	20	25	30	35	40	45	50
6	6	12	18	24	30	36	42	48	54	60
7	7	14	21	28	35	42	49	56	63	70
8	8	16	24	32	40	48	56	64	72	80
9	9	18	27	36	45	54	63	72	81	90
10	10	20	30	40	50	60	70	80	90	100

5. Describe the pattern you see in the table for multiples of 5 and 10.

Possible Answer: The row and column for the multiples of 5 show that they all end in 5 or 0, and the row and column for multiples of 10 show that they all end in 0.

6. Which is true for all the products of 9 × 1 through 9 × 10?

(A) When you multiply 9 and an odd number, the product is an even number.

(B) The digit in the tens place is 1 less each time the factor increases by 1.

(C) When you multiply 9 and an even number, the product is an odd number.

● The digit in the ones place and the digit in the tens place add up to 9.

7. How does the table show that the product of 8 × 7 is the same as the product 7 × 8?

Possible Answer: Find the row for 8 and the column for 7. The number in the square where the row and column meet is the product, 56. Then, find the product of 7 and 8 by finding the row for 7 and the column for 8. The number in the square where the row and column meet is also the product, 56. So, the order of the factors 8 and 7 does not change their product.

8. Write the missing numbers in the table. Then, tell what the rule is.

IN	12	16	30	34	44	50	60
OUT	6	8	15	17	22	25	30

The rule is divide by 2.

73

Round Numbers to the Nearest 10 or 100
Numbers and Operations

DIRECTIONS: Choose or write the correct answer.

Strategy — Apply the rules for rounding to the nearest 10 or 100 when using basic operations that ask for estimates.

Test Tip — Look for key words when solving a problem. If the word *about* is used, an exact answer may not be necessary.

EXAMPLE:

Find the sum of 73 + 48 by rounding the numbers to the nearest 10. Which is correct?

(A) 100 + 40
(B) 100 + 50
(C) 70 + 40
(D) 70 + 50

Answer: D

1. Which of these is the best way to find the answer to this problem by rounding to the nearest 10?

28 − 19 = ☐

(A) 30 − 10
(B) 20 − 10
● 30 − 20
(D) 10 − 10

2. Round each number to the nearest 10 to find which of the sums is close to 100. Choose all that apply.

(A) 59 + 57
● 51 + 49
(C) 39 + 58
● 91 + 8

3. Some people brought their pets to an animal fair. 133 people brought dogs. 180 people brought cats. 110 people brought other pets. About how many people brought pets to the fair? Solve the problem by rounding the numbers to the nearest 100. Show your work.

400 people; 100 + 200 + 100 = 400

4. What is 34,571 rounded to the nearest 100?

(A) 34,000
(B) 35,500
● 34,600
(D) 34,570

5. Lisa, Jana, and Corey weighed pumpkins they had grown during the summer. The weights are shown in the table below. To the nearest 100, about how much do the pumpkins weigh all together? Show how you know.

Lisa's Pumpkin	184 pounds
Jana's Pumpkin	289 pounds
Corey's Pumpkin	304 pounds

Possible Answer: about 800 pounds; round 184 to 200; round 289 to 300; round 304 to 300; then, add: 200 + 300 + 300 = 800; or add the original numbers to get a sum of 777 and round it to the nearest 100, which is 800.

74

Round Numbers to the Nearest 10 or 100
Numbers and Operations

DIRECTIONS: Choose or write the correct answer.

Strategy — Use the rules for rounding up or down as you solve problems requiring estimation.

Test Tip — When rounding to the nearest 100, if the value of the number in the tens place is less than 5, round the number down.

6. Josela collected 578 plastic water bottles to recycle.

578 rounded to the nearest 10 is ___580___.

7. Look at the numbers in the box below. Which number, when rounded to the nearest 100, rounds to 600? Write how you know.

498, 579, 668, 536

579; To round to hundreds, look at the tens place. Because 7 tens is more than 5 tens, add 1 to the 5 in the hundreds place and drop the other numbers, or, because 579 is more than halfway between 500 and 600, round up to 600.

8. Round to the tens and hundreds place. Write each number in the correct box.

Number	Rounded to the Nearest 10	Rounded to the Nearest 100
315	320	300
1,068	1,070	1,000
72	70	100
for example, 342	340	300

9. Mr. Ames is the grocery store manager. He counts all the customers that come into the store one day and rounds the number to the closest hundred. He rounds to 800. Which of these could be the original number of customers? Choose all that apply.

● 831
(B) 897
● 767
(D) 749

75

Add and Subtract Within 1,000
Numbers and Operations

DIRECTIONS: Choose or write the correct answer.

Strategy — When adding and subtracting larger numbers, line them up by place value to make sure your answer is correct.

EXAMPLE

There are 134 students on the playground and 254 students inside the school. What is the total number of students?

One way to add:
100 + 200 = 300
30 + 50 = 80
4 + 4 = 8
300 + 80 + 8 = 388 students

1. What is the missing number in this number sentence?

248 + 672 = ☐

(A) 224
(B) 324
● 920
(D) 334

2. A truck driver makes deliveries between two cities. The cities are 534 miles apart. He has already driven 165 miles. How many more miles does he have to go?

(A) 431 miles
(B) 469 miles
(C) 489 miles
● 369 miles

Test Tip — Check your answer to see if it makes sense.

3. Jeffrey explained how to add 168 and 115. He made a mistake. What mistake did Jeffrey make?

Jeffrey's Way

• Add 2 to 168 to get 170.
• Add 110 to 170 to get 280.
• The sum is 280.

Possible Answer: Jeffrey forgot to add the 3 leftover to get a sum of 283.

4. The number of people watching a high school football game is 732. At half time, 56 people leave. How many people are left watching the game?

(A) 724 people
(B) 684 people
● 676 people
(D) 686 people

5. Callie, Alyssa, and Nina count stickers in their collections. The numbers are shown in the table below. How many stickers do the girls have all together? Show how you know.

Callie's Stickers	38
Alyssa's Stickers	115
Nina's Stickers	89

Possible Answer: 242 stickers; add 38 + 115 + 89; the sum is 242.

76

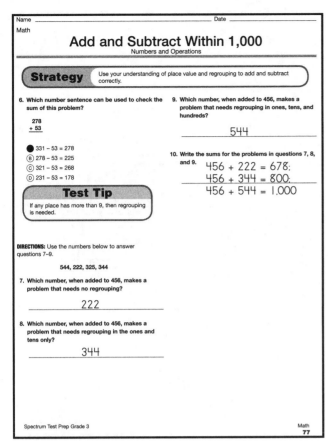

Name _____ Date _____
Math

Add and Subtract Within 1,000
Numbers and Operations

Strategy Use your understanding of place value and regrouping to add and subtract correctly.

6. Which number sentence can be used to check the sum of this problem?

278
+ 53

● 331 – 53 = 278
Ⓑ 278 – 53 = 225
Ⓒ 321 – 53 = 268
Ⓓ 231 – 53 = 178

Test Tip
If any place has more than 9, then regrouping is needed.

DIRECTIONS: Use the numbers below to answer questions 7–9.

544, 222, 325, 344

7. Which number, when added to 456, makes a problem that needs no regrouping?

222

8. Which number, when added to 456, makes a problem that needs regrouping in the ones and tens only?

344

9. Which number, when added to 456, makes a problem that needs regrouping in ones, tens, and hundreds?

544

10. Write the sums for the problems in questions 7, 8, and 9.

456 + 222 = 678;
456 + 344 = 800;
456 + 544 = 1,000

Spectrum Test Prep Grade 3
Math 77

77

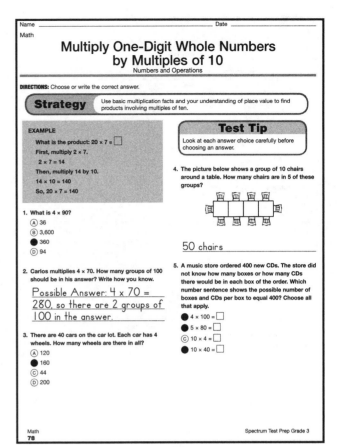

Name _____ Date _____
Math

Multiply One-Digit Whole Numbers by Multiples of 10
Numbers and Operations

DIRECTIONS: Choose or write the correct answer.

Strategy Use basic multiplication facts and your understanding of place value to find products involving multiples of ten.

EXAMPLE
What is the product: 20 × 7 = ☐
First, multiply 2 × 7.
2 × 7 = 14
Then, multiply 14 by 10.
14 × 10 = 140
So, 20 × 7 = 140

1. What is 4 × 90?
Ⓐ 36
Ⓑ 3,600
● 360
Ⓓ 94

2. Carlos multiplies 4 × 70. How many groups of 100 should be in his answer? Write how you know.

Possible Answer: 4 × 70 = 280, so there are 2 groups of 100 in the answer.

3. There are 40 cars on the car lot. Each car has 4 wheels. How many wheels are there in all?
Ⓐ 120
● 160
Ⓒ 44
Ⓓ 200

Test Tip
Look at each answer choice carefully before choosing an answer.

4. The picture below shows a group of 10 chairs around a table. How many chairs are in 5 of these groups?

50 chairs

5. A music store ordered 400 new CDs. The store did not know how many boxes or how many CDs there would be in each box of the order. Which number sentence shows the possible number of boxes and CDs per box to equal 400? Choose all that apply.
● 4 × 100 = ☐
● 5 × 80 = ☐
Ⓒ 10 × 4 = ☐
● 10 × 40 = ☐

Math 78
Spectrum Test Prep Grade 3

78

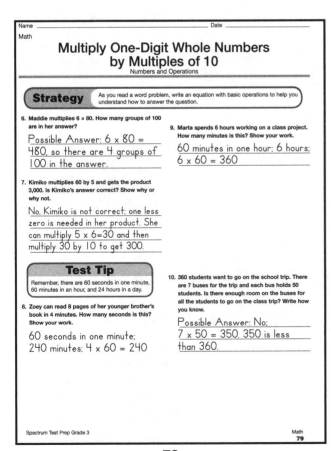

Name _____ Date _____
Math

Multiply One-Digit Whole Numbers by Multiples of 10
Numbers and Operations

Strategy As you read a word problem, write an equation with basic operations to help you understand how to answer the question.

6. Maddie multiplies 6 × 80. How many groups of 100 are in her answer?

Possible Answer: 6 × 80 = 480, so there are 4 groups of 100 in the answer.

7. Kimiko multiplies 60 by 5 and gets the product 3,000. Is Kimiko's answer correct? Show why or why not.

No, Kimiko is not correct; one less zero is needed in her product. She can multiply 5 × 6=30 and then multiply 30 by 10 to get 300.

Test Tip
Remember, there are 60 seconds in one minute, 60 minutes in an hour, and 24 hours in a day.

8. Zoey can read 8 pages of her younger brother's book in 4 minutes. How many seconds is this? Show your work.

60 seconds in one minute; 240 minutes; 4 × 60 = 240

9. Marta spends 6 hours working on a class project. How many minutes is this? Show your work.

60 minutes in one hour; 6 hours; 6 × 60 = 360

10. 360 students want to go on the school trip. There are 7 buses for the trip and each bus holds 50 students. Is there enough room on the buses for all the students to go on the class trip? Write how you know.

Possible Answer: No;
7 × 50 = 350. 350 is less than 360.

Spectrum Test Prep Grade 3
Math 79

79

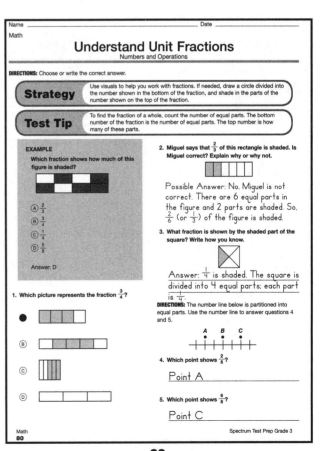

Name _____ Date _____
Math

Understand Unit Fractions
Numbers and Operations

DIRECTIONS: Choose or write the correct answer.

Strategy Use visuals to help you work with fractions. If needed, draw a circle divided into the number shown in the bottom of the fraction, and shade in the parts of the number shown on the top of the fraction.

Test Tip To find the fraction of a whole, count the number of equal parts. The bottom number of the fraction is the number of equal parts. The top number is how many of these parts.

EXAMPLE
Which fraction shows how much of this figure is shaded?

Ⓐ $\frac{2}{3}$
Ⓑ $\frac{3}{4}$
Ⓒ $\frac{1}{4}$
Ⓓ $\frac{5}{8}$

Answer: D

1. Which picture represents the fraction $\frac{3}{4}$?
● (A)
Ⓑ
Ⓒ
Ⓓ

2. Miguel says that $\frac{2}{3}$ of this rectangle is shaded. Is Miguel correct? Explain why or why not.

Possible Answer: No, Miguel is not correct. There are 6 equal parts in the figure and 2 parts are shaded. So, $\frac{2}{6}$ (or $\frac{1}{3}$) of the figure is shaded.

3. What fraction is shown by the shaded part of the square? Write how you know.

Answer: $\frac{1}{4}$ is shaded. The square is divided into 4 equal parts; each part is $\frac{1}{4}$.

DIRECTIONS: The number line below is partitioned into equal parts. Use the number line to answer questions 4 and 5.

4. Which point shows $\frac{2}{8}$?

Point A

5. Which point shows $\frac{6}{8}$?

Point C

Math 80
Spectrum Test Prep Grade 3

80

Understand Unit Fractions
Numbers and Operations

Strategy Use pictures as tools that you can use to solve fractions. Study a picture carefully to be sure you understand what it represents.

6. Which fraction is shown by the unshaded part of the circle?

● A. $\frac{4}{6}$

B. $\frac{2}{6}$

C. $\frac{1}{6}$

D. $\frac{6}{6}$

7. Which rectangle is divided into fourths? Choose all that apply.

●

B.

●

●

DIRECTIONS: Use the pictures of the pizzas below to answer questions 8 and 9.

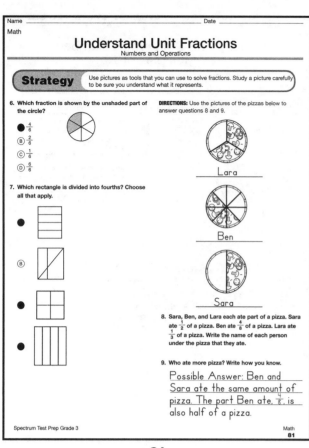

Lara

Ben

Sara

8. Sara, Ben, and Lara each ate part of a pizza. Sara ate $\frac{1}{2}$ of a pizza. Ben ate $\frac{4}{8}$ of a pizza. Lara ate $\frac{1}{3}$ of a pizza. Write the name of each person under the pizza that they ate.

9. Who ate more pizza? Write how you know.

<u>Possible Answer: Ben and Sara ate the same amount of pizza. The part Ben ate, $\frac{4}{8}$, is also half of a pizza.</u>

81

Represent Fractions on a Number Line
Numbers and Operations

DIRECTIONS: Choose or write the correct answer.

Strategy Use graphs, tables, and drawings to understand data.

1. Tomas and Fabio were sharing one pizza. Tomas ate $\frac{3}{8}$ of the pizza and Fabio ate $\frac{5}{8}$. Tomas drew the number line below to show how much he and Fabio ate. Is the number line correct? Write how you know.

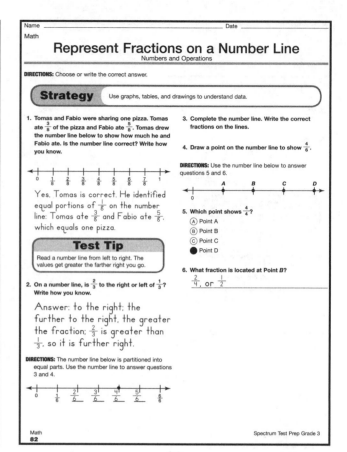

<u>Yes, Tomas is correct. He identified equal portions of $\frac{1}{8}$ on the number line: Tomas ate $\frac{3}{8}$ and Fabio ate $\frac{5}{8}$, which equals one pizza.</u>

Test Tip
Read a number line from left to right. The values get greater the farther right you go.

2. On a number line, is $\frac{2}{3}$ to the right or left of $\frac{1}{3}$? Write how you know.

<u>Answer: to the right; the further to the right, the greater the fraction; $\frac{2}{3}$ is greater than $\frac{1}{3}$, so it is further right.</u>

DIRECTIONS: The number line below is partitioned into equal parts. Use the number line to answer questions 3 and 4.

3. Complete the number line. Write the correct fractions on the lines.

4. Draw a point on the number line to show $\frac{4}{6}$.

DIRECTIONS: Use the number line below to answer questions 5 and 6.

5. Which point shows $\frac{4}{4}$?

A. Point A

B. Point B

C. Point C

● Point D

6. What fraction is located at Point B?

$\frac{2}{4}$, or $\frac{1}{2}$

82

Represent Fractions on a Number Line
Numbers and Operations

DIRECTIONS: Use the number line below to answer questions 7–9.

Strategy Use number lines as tools to help you read fractions.

Test Tip To read fractions on a number line, count the equal intervals between 0 and 1.

$\frac{2}{3}$

7. Van cut his fruit bar into thirds. He ate 2 of the 3 parts of the bar. Draw a point on the number line to show the part of the fruit bar Van ate.

8. Write the fraction above the point.

9. Write why you placed the point where you did.

<u>Possible Answer: There are 3 equal parts on the number line between 0 and 1. Van ate 2 of the 3 parts of the bar, or $\frac{2}{3}$ of the bar, so the point is placed at $\frac{2}{3}$, which is at the end of the second part.</u>

10. Neal and Lars are sharing the duty of cutting their family's lawn. Neal cuts $\frac{2}{6}$ of the lawn and Lars cuts $\frac{4}{6}$ of the lawn. Which number line correctly shows the fractional amount each boy cuts?

● A. Neal   Lars

B. Neal   Lars

C. Lars   Neal

D. Neal   Lars

83

Use Fraction Models and Number Lines to Generate Equivalent Fractions
Numbers and Operations

DIRECTIONS: Choose or write the correct answer.

Strategy Look at the shaded parts of graphs, tables, and drawings to understand parts of a whole.

1. The shape below has $\frac{1}{3}$ shaded. Which shape has a shaded amount equal to $\frac{1}{3}$?

●

B.

C.

D.

DIRECTIONS: Use the information below to answer questions 2–5.

Isabel plants a flower garden and a vegetable garden of equal size. She plants $\frac{2}{4}$ of her flower garden with daisies and $\frac{4}{8}$ of her vegetable garden with peppers.

2. Shade the rectangle to show how much of Isabel's flower garden is planted with daisies.

3. Shade the rectangle to show how much of Isabel's vegetable garden is planted with peppers.

4. Write a number sentence using <, =, or > to compare the fraction of the flower garden that is planted with daisies and the fraction of the vegetable garden that is planted with peppers.

$\frac{2}{4}$ = $\frac{4}{8}$

5. Write how you know your number sentence is correct.

Possible Answer: The two rectangles I shaded are the same size, and the same amounts are shaded. So I know that $\frac{2}{4} = \frac{4}{8}$.

84

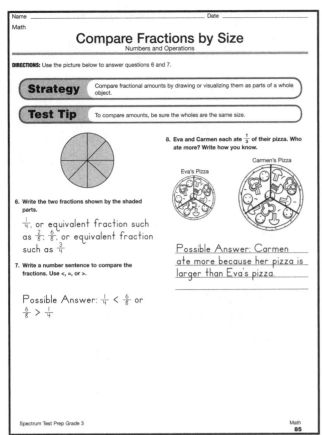

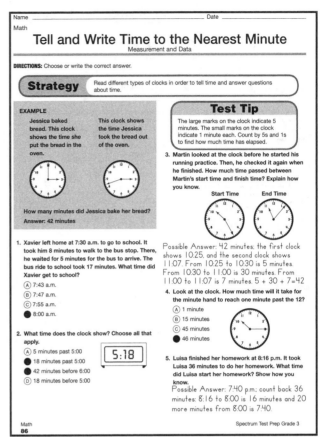

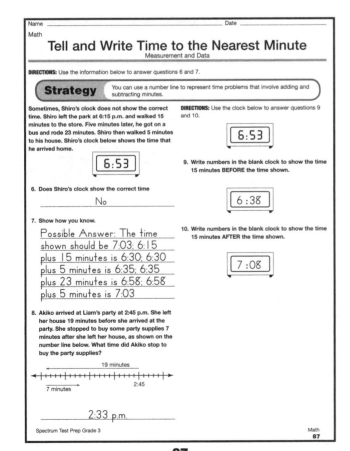

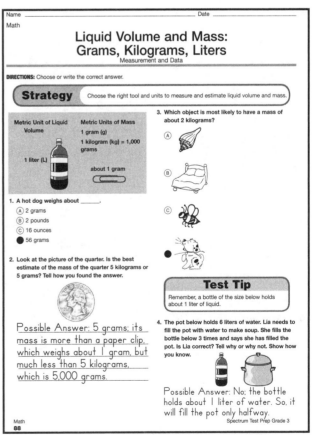

Solve One-Step Problems: Mass and Volume
Measurement and Data

DIRECTIONS: Choose or write the correct answer.

Strategy Use basic operations to solve problems involving measurements. Read the problems carefully to decide which operation to use. Draw pictures if needed.

1. Lila has 4 new pencils that together weigh 20 grams. How much does one pencil weigh?
   - Ⓐ 4 grams
   - ● 5 grams
   - Ⓒ 15 grams
   - Ⓓ 20 grams

2. Bennett buys 4 watermelons with the same mass as the one shown below. What is the mass of the 4 watermelons Bennett buys? Show how you know.

   mass = 4 kg

   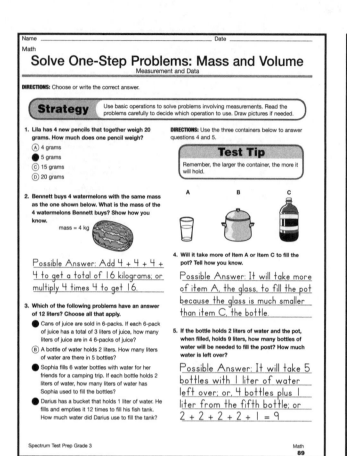

   Possible Answer: Add 4 + 4 + 4 + 4 to get a total of 16 kilograms; or multiply 4 times 4 to get 16.

3. Which of the following problems have an answer of 12 liters? Choose all that apply.
   - ● Cans of juice are sold in 6-packs. If each 6-pack of juice has a total of 3 liters of juice, how many liters of juice are in 4 6-packs of juice?
   - Ⓑ A bottle of water holds 2 liters. How many liters of water are there in 5 bottles?
   - ● Sophia fills 6 water bottles with water for her friends for a camping trip. If each bottle holds 2 liters of water, how many liters of water has Sophia used to fill the bottles?
   - ● Darius has a bucket that holds 1 liter of water. He fills and empties it 12 times to fill his fish tank. How much water did Darius use to fill the tank?

DIRECTIONS: Use the three containers below to answer questions 4 and 5.

Test Tip
Remember, the larger the container, the more it will hold.

A   B   C

4. Will it take more of Item A or Item C to fill the pot? Tell how you know.

   Possible Answer: It will take more of item A, the glass, to fill the pot because the glass is much smaller than item C, the bottle.

5. If the bottle holds 2 liters of water and the pot, when filled, holds 9 liters, how many bottles of water will be needed to fill the post? How much water is left over?

   Possible Answer: It will take 5 bottles with 1 liter of water left over; or, 4 bottles plus 1 liter from the fifth bottle; or 2 + 2 + 2 + 2 + 1 = 9

Draw Picture Graphs and Bar Graphs
Measurement and Data

DIRECTIONS: Choose or write the correct answer.

Strategy When viewing graphs, tables, and drawings, read the labels and captions carefully to make sure you understand the data shown.

Test Tip A scaled pictograph includes symbols that represent multiple units. In a scaled bar graph, each interval also represents multiple units, such as 5.

1. The data in the table below shows a person's heart rate while jogging. Use the data to complete the bar graph. Draw bars to show the data.

Time	Heart Rate
0 min.	80
5 min.	120
10 min.	130
15 min.	150
20 min.	160
25 min.	150

   Bar Graph
   Heart Rate While Jogging

   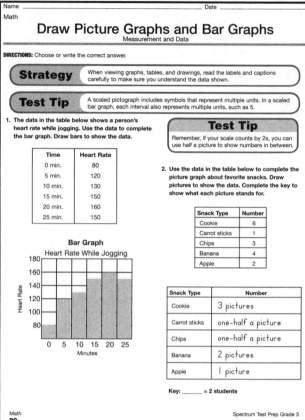

2. Use the data in the table below to complete the picture graph about favorite snacks. Draw pictures to show the data. Complete the key to show what each picture stands for.

Snack Type	Number
Cookie	6
Carrot sticks	1
Chips	3
Banana	4
Apple	2

Snack Type	Number
Cookie	3 pictures
Carrot sticks	one-half a picture
Chips	one-half a picture
Banana	2 pictures
Apple	1 picture

   Key: _____ = 2 students

Solve Problems Using Bar Graphs
Measurement and Data

Strategy If you don't understand the data in a graph, table, or drawing, take the information and try drawing a different visual. Or, make a table with the information.

DIRECTIONS: Use the bar graph below to answer questions 1–3.

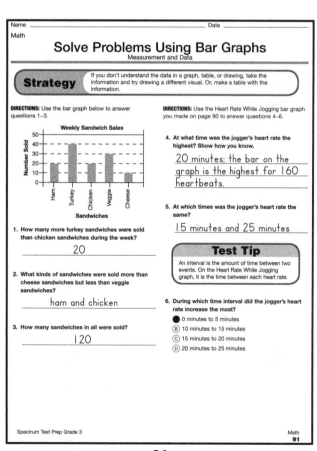

Weekly Sandwich Sales

1. How many more turkey sandwiches were sold than chicken sandwiches during the week?

   20

2. What kinds of sandwiches were sold more than cheese sandwiches but less than veggie sandwiches?

   ham and chicken

3. How many sandwiches in all were sold?

   120

DIRECTIONS: Use the Heart Rate While Jogging bar graph you made on page 90 to answer questions 4–6.

4. At what time was the jogger's heart rate the highest? Show how you know.

   20 minutes; the bar on the graph is the highest for 160 heartbeats.

5. At which times was the jogger's heart rate the same?

   15 minutes and 25 minutes

Test Tip
An interval is the amount of time between two events. On the Heart Rate While Jogging graph, it is the time between each heart rate.

6. During which time interval did the jogger's heart rate increase the most?
   - ● 0 minutes to 5 minutes
   - Ⓑ 10 minutes to 15 minutes
   - Ⓒ 15 minutes to 20 minutes
   - Ⓓ 20 minutes to 25 minutes

Measure Length and Show Data on a Line Plot
Measurement and Data

DIRECTIONS: Choose or write the correct answer.

Strategy Look for what graphs, tables, and drawings are comparing. Most graphs and tables compare more than one object.

1. Zuri has some lengths of ribbon that she will weave together. The ribbons are shown below. Measure the lengths in inches and write the measures.

   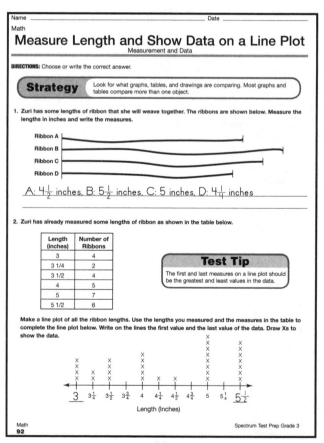

   Ribbon A
   Ribbon B
   Ribbon C
   Ribbon D

   A: $4\frac{1}{2}$ inches, B: $5\frac{1}{2}$ inches, C: 5 inches, D: $4\frac{1}{4}$ inches

2. Zuri has already measured some lengths of ribbon as shown in the table below.

Length (inches)	Number of Ribbons
3	4
3 1/4	2
3 1/2	4
4	5
5	7
5 1/2	6

   Test Tip
   The first and last measures on a line plot should be the greatest and least values in the data.

   Make a line plot of all the ribbon lengths. Use the lengths you measured and the measures in the table to complete the line plot below. Write on the lines the first value and the last value of the data. Draw Xs to show the data.

   Length (Inches)

Finding Area: Unit Squares
Measurement and Data

DIRECTIONS: Choose or write the correct answer.

Strategy
Use unit squares to find area.

EXAMPLE
The area of a figure can be found by finding the total number of same-size units of area required to cover the shape without gaps or overlaps. The area of the figure below is 4 square units.

← 1 square unit

Test Tip
Count the square units to find the area.

1. What is the area of this figure?

- (A) 14 square units
- (B) 16 square units
- (C) 22 square units
- ● 18 square units

DIRECTIONS: Look at the figure below. The side of each square represents 1 inch. Use the figure to answer questions 2–4.

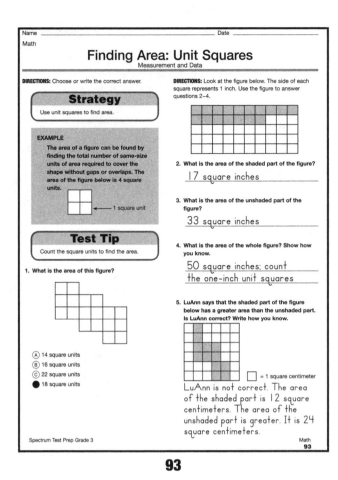

2. What is the area of the shaded part of the figure?

17 square inches

3. What is the area of the unshaded part of the figure?

33 square inches

4. What is the area of the whole figure? Show how you know.

50 square inches; count the one-inch unit squares

5. LuAnn says that the shaded part of the figure below has a greater area than the unshaded part. Is LuAnn correct? Write how you know.

☐ = 1 square centimeter

LuAnn is not correct. The area of the shaded part is 12 square centimeters. The area of the unshaded part is greater. It is 24 square centimeters.

Relate Finding Area to Multiplication and Addition
Measurement and Data

DIRECTIONS: Choose or write the correct answer.

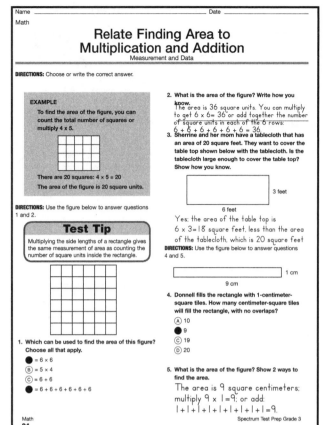

EXAMPLE
To find the area of the figure, you can count the total number of squares or multiply 4 x 5.

There are 20 squares: 4 x 5 = 20
The area of the figure is 20 square units.

DIRECTIONS: Use the figure below to answer questions 1 and 2.

Test Tip
Multiplying the side lengths of a rectangle gives the same measurement of area as counting the number of square units inside the rectangle.

1. Which can be used to find the area of this figure? Choose all that apply.

- ● 6 x 6
- (B) 5 x 4
- (C) 6 + 6
- ● 6 + 6 + 6 + 6 + 6 + 6

2. What is the area of the figure? Write how you know.

The area is 36 square units. You can multiply to get 6 x 6 = 36 or add together the number of square units in each of the 6 rows: 6 + 6 + 6 + 6 + 6 + 6 = 36.

3. Sherrine and her mom have a tablecloth that has an area of 20 square feet. They want to cover the table top shown below with the tablecloth. Is the tablecloth large enough to cover the table top? Show how you know.

3 feet

6 feet

Yes; the area of the table top is 6 x 3 = 18 square feet, less than the area of the tablecloth, which is 20 square feet.

DIRECTIONS: Use the figure below to answer questions 4 and 5.

1 cm

9 cm

4. Donnell fills the rectangle with 1-centimeter-square tiles. How many centimeter-square tiles will fill the rectangle, with no overlaps?

- (A) 10
- ● 9
- (C) 19
- (D) 20

5. What is the area of the figure? Show 2 ways to find the area.

The area is 9 square centimeters; multiply 9 x 1 = 9; or add: 1 + 1 + 1 + 1 + 1 + 1 + 1 + 1 + 1 = 9.

Relate Finding Area to Multiplication and Addition
Measurement and Data

DIRECTIONS: Choose or write the correct answer.

Strategy
Use multiplication and addition to find the areas of figures in square units.

DIRECTIONS: Mr. Miller drew the figure below on the board. Use the figure to answer questions 6 and 7.

6. Levon says the area of the figure is 18 square units. He counted the squares around the outside of the figure. Mr. Miller tells Levon he did not find the area of the figure correctly. What did Levon do wrong? Include the correct area in your answer.

Possible Answer: Levon must count all the unit squares in the figure to find the area, not just those on the outside There are 30 squares all together. So, the area is 30 square units.

7. Show how you can use multiplication to find the area of Mr. Miller's figure.

Possible Answer: There are 6 rows with 5 squares in each row, so 6 x 5 = 30.

Test Tip
You can find the area of some figures by separating them into non-overlapping rectangles and adding together the areas of the non-overlapping rectangles.

8. Alyssa wrote a number sentence to find the area of her figure. The number sentence uses multiplication and addition. Write the number sentence Alyssa could have written.

Possible Answer:
(3 x 2) + (3 x 2) + (3 x 2) = 18

Solve Problems: Perimeter
Measurement and Data

DIRECTIONS: Choose or write the correct answer.

Strategy
Use addition to find the perimeters of figures. Identify the number of sides a figure has and the length of each side. Then, add to find the perimeter.

EXAMPLE
Perimeter is the distance around the edge of a shape.
You can add to find the perimeter.

Width = 5 ft

Length = 18 ft

5 + 5 + 18 + 18 = 46
The perimeter is 46 feet.

Test Tip
Add the lengths of the four sides to find the perimeter.

1. A rectangle has a length of 27 feet and a width of 2 feet. What is the perimeter?

- (A) 27 feet
- ● 58 feet
- (C) 29 feet
- (D) 54 feet

2. A rectangle has a perimeter of 24 feet. Which can be the side measures of the rectangle? Choose all that apply.

- ● length: 10 feet; width 2 feet
- ● length: 11 feet; width 1 foot
- (C) length: 12 feet; width 3 feet
- ● length: 7 feet; width 5 feet

3. The triangle below has a perimeter of 37 inches. What is the length of the bottom of the triangle? Show how you found your answer.

16 in.   16 in.

? inches

The length is 5 inches;
16 + 16 = 32; 37 – 32 = 5

Test Tip
To find the perimeter of a rectangle, you can double the lengths of the sides next to each other and then, add them together.

4. Jack drew two rectangles, A and B, shown below. They have the same perimeter. Jack says they also have the same area. Is Jack correct? Show how you know.

4 meters

5 meters

3 meters

6 meters

No, Jack is not correct. The perimeter of each rectangle is 18 meters. But, the area of A is 20 square meters and the area of B is 18 square meters.

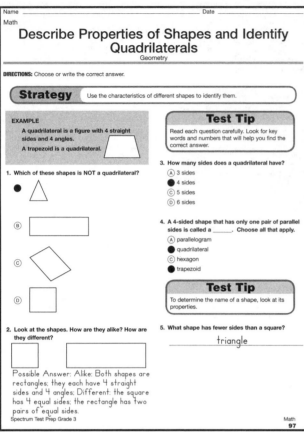

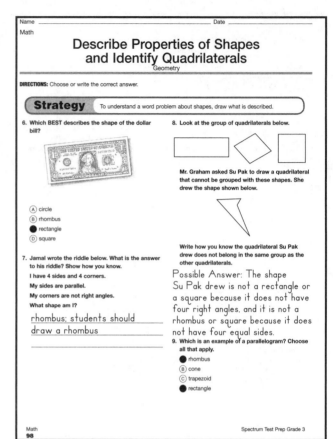

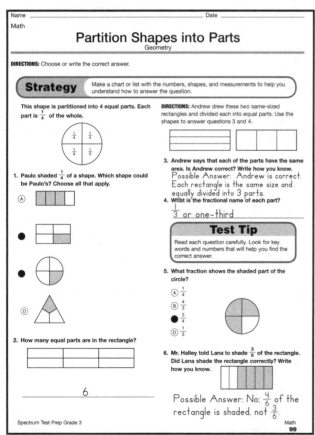

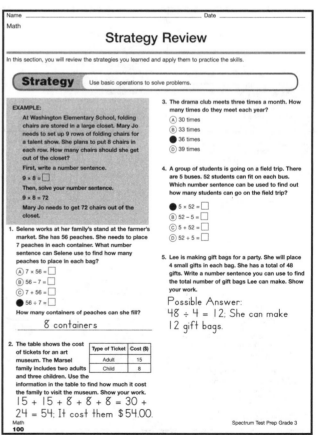

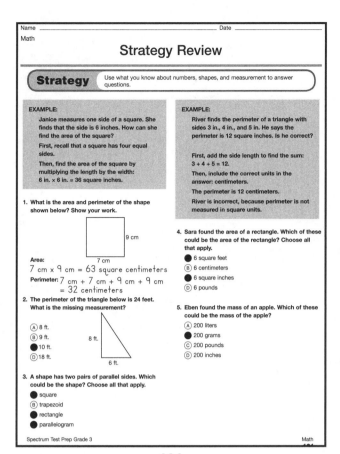

Page 101

Name _____ Date _____
Math

Strategy Review

Strategy Use what you know about numbers, shapes, and measurement to answer questions.

EXAMPLE:

Janice measures one side of a square. She finds that the side is 6 inches. How can she find the area of the square?

First, recall that a square has four equal sides.

Then, find the area of the square by multiplying the length by the width:
6 in. × 6 in. = 36 square inches.

EXAMPLE:

River finds the perimeter of a triangle with sides 3 in., 4 in., and 5 in. He says the perimeter is 12 square inches. Is he correct?

First, add the side length to find the sum:
3 + 4 + 5 = 12.

Then, include the correct units in the answer: centimeters.

The perimeter is 12 centimeters.

River is incorrect, because perimeter is not measured in square units.

1. What is the area and perimeter of the shape shown below? Show your work.

9 cm
7 cm

Area:
7 cm × 9 cm = 63 square centimeters
Perimeter: 7 cm + 7 cm + 9 cm + 9 cm = 32 centimeters

2. The perimeter of the triangle below is 24 feet. What is the missing measurement?

Ⓐ 8 ft.
Ⓑ 9 ft.
● 10 ft.
Ⓓ 18 ft.

8 ft.
6 ft.

3. A shape has two pairs of parallel sides. Which could be the shape? Choose all that apply.

● square
Ⓑ trapezoid
● rectangle
● parallelogram

4. Sara found the area of a rectangle. Which of these could be the area of the rectangle? Choose all that apply.

● 6 square feet
Ⓑ 6 centimeters
● 6 square inches
Ⓓ 6 pounds

5. Eben found the mass of an apple. Which of these could be the mass of the apple?

Ⓐ 200 liters
● 200 grams
Ⓒ 200 pounds
Ⓓ 200 inches

Spectrum Test Prep Grade 3   Math 101

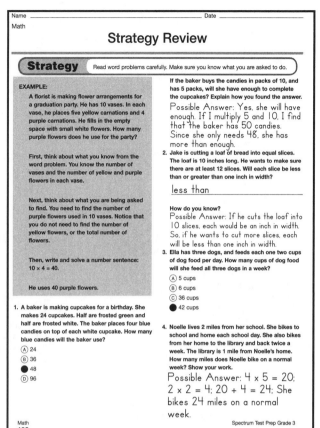

Page 102

Name _____ Date _____
Math

Strategy Review

Strategy Read word problems carefully. Make sure you know what you are asked to do.

EXAMPLE:

A florist is making flower arrangements for a graduation party. He has 10 vases. In each vase, he places five yellow carnations and 4 purple carnations. He fills in the empty space with small white flowers. How many purple flowers does he use for the party?

First, think about what you know from the word problem. You know the number of vases and the number of yellow and purple flowers in each vase.

Next, think about what you are being asked to find. You need to find the number of purple flowers used in 10 vases. Notice that you do not need to find the number of yellow flowers, or the total number of flowers.

Then, write and solve a number sentence:
10 × 4 = 40.

He uses 40 purple flowers.

1. A baker is making cupcakes for a birthday. She makes 24 cupcakes. Half are frosted green and half are frosted white. The baker places four blue candies on top of each white cupcake. How many blue candies will the baker use?

Ⓐ 24
Ⓑ 36
● 48
Ⓓ 96

If the baker buys the candies in packs of 10, and has 5 packs, will she have enough to complete the cupcakes? Explain how you found the answer.

Possible Answer: Yes, she will have enough. If I multiply 5 and 10, I find that the baker has 50 candies. Since she only needs 48, she has more than enough.

2. Jake is cutting a loaf of bread into equal slices. The loaf is 10 inches long. He wants to make sure there are at least 12 slices. Will each slice be less than or greater than one inch in width?

less than

How do you know?
Possible Answer: If he cuts the loaf into 10 slices, each would be an inch in width. So, if he wants to cut more slices, each will be less than one inch in width.

3. Ella has three dogs, and feeds each one two cups of dog food per day. How many cups of dog food will she feed all three dogs in a week?

Ⓐ 5 cups
Ⓑ 6 cups
Ⓒ 36 cups
● 42 cups

4. Noelle lives 2 miles from her school. She bikes to school and home each school day. She also bikes from her home to the library and back twice a week. The library is 1 mile from Noelle's home. How many miles does Noelle bike on a normal week? Show your work.

Possible Answer: 4 × 5 = 20; 2 × 2 = 4; 20 + 4 = 24; She bikes 24 miles on a normal week.

Math 102   Spectrum Test Prep Grade 3

Page 103

Name _____ Date _____
Math

Strategy Review

Strategy Use graphs, tables, and drawings to understand numbers.

EXAMPLE

Shana has 1 pound of butter. She uses $\frac{1}{2}$ pound to make biscuits. She used another $\frac{1}{4}$ pound for a pie crust. How much butter did she use? Shade the rectangle to show how much she used. Then, use your shaded rectangle to find how much was left.

First, shade in the fraction of the butter that she used for the biscuits:

Then, shade in the fraction she used for the pie:

She used $\frac{3}{4}$ pound of butter.
$\frac{1}{4}$ pound was left.

1. Lorne drew the number line below to solve a problem.

0   1

Which of the following could be the problem Lorne solved?

Ⓐ A teacher made 2 gallons of lemonade. He used $\frac{1}{2}$ gallon to fill cups for the students. How much lemonade was left?
● A teacher made 1 gallon of lemonade. He used $\frac{2}{3}$ gallon to fill cups for the students. How much lemonade was left?
Ⓒ A teacher made 2 gallons of lemonade. He used $\frac{2}{3}$ gallon to fill cups for the students. How much lemonade was left?
Ⓓ A teacher made 1 gallon of lemonade. He used $\frac{1}{2}$ gallon to fill cups for the students. How much lemonade was left?

2. Jay, Maddy, and Evan share two pizzas. Each pizza is cut into 6 equal pieces. Maddy eats three pieces, Jay eats two pieces, and Evan eats three pieces. How many pieces of pizza are left? Draw a picture to help you find an answer.

4 pieces are left. Pictures should show 2 pizzas, each cut into 6 pieces, with a total of 8 pieces shaded and 4 pieces unshaded.

3. Eric and Toby each ordered a sandwich. Eric ate $\frac{2}{3}$ of his sandwich. Toby ate $\frac{3}{4}$ of his sandwich. Who ate a greater amount of his sandwich? Draw a picture and show your work.

Toby ate a greater amount of his sandwich. Any illustration that compares $\frac{2}{3}$ with $\frac{4}{5}$ is acceptable.

4. Mr. and Mrs. Barrett are painting their basement walls. On Tuesday, they painted $\frac{1}{3}$ of the walls. On Wednesday, they painted $\frac{1}{3}$ more of the walls. If they want to finish the job on Thursday, what fraction of the walls will they need to paint? Draw a picture and show your work.

They need to paint $\frac{1}{3}$ of the walls. Pictures may show a rectangle or circle divided into thirds

Spectrum Test Prep Grade 3   Math 103
